God's Way and Finances

The Kingdom of God's Economic System vs. the World's Economy

AUDREY L. DICKEY, PH.D.

Kingdom Advance Publishing
P. O. Box 48288
Los Angeles, California 90048
877.333.5075

robertandaudreydickeyministries.org

Printed in the United States of America
ISBN: 978-0-9997611-6-8

Library of Congress Control Number: 2018903048
Kingdom Advance Publishing, Los Angeles, CA

Christian Life / Business & Economics

DEDICATION

To my cousin, Gail, who is truly a blessing in my life! You are a faithful and diligent person.

Once you discovered there were two economic systems operating on the earth you quickly jumped on board to honor God. Because you chose to steward what was entrusted to you God's Way, you have seen His faithfulness firsthand and discovered the heavens opened with favor, revelation and increase.

You are successful, an example of integrity and a true servant of the Lord. Gail, you have a beautiful and giving heart, may the Lord continue to richly bless your life! Love you Gail!

CONTENTS

INTRODUCTION

I was encouraged by Holy Spirit many years ago to write. It was confirmed numerous times. Over the years I have gathered research and along with personal experiences now the series mandate is fulfilled.

In this financial resource and tool not only will you learn the difference between God's Economic System and the World's Economic System you will receive a new perspective on how you perceive money. Plus, you will acquire a change from the world's perception of money and their purpose for it. We will also discuss ways to activate the anointing of Multiplication to operate in a Believer's life.

This information and revelation will also enlighten the readers and alert them to the fact *they cannot serve two masters,* "You cannot serve God and mammon (deceitful riches, money, possessions, or whatever is trusted in)," Matthew 6:24.

There are two economic systems in the world, the Kingdom of God's and the world's (those not in covenant with God nor are they a part of His family). *People will need to decide which one they are going to serve (worship).*

If you are a child of the King, the Anointed Messiah, then you have no recourse but to follow

Him through the leading of His Holy Spirit and His written Word.

Those who chose to compromise will only short change themselves from the fullness of His glory (presence) in this season.

Furthermore, a *major shift* in God's Kingdom within His church has occurred. The glory of God on the earth will begin to increase at an accelerated pace with power we have not seen before.

Wealth is attached to His glory. The wealth that has been stored up by sinners, those of the world without covenant, is for the righteous, those that are in Christ Messiah, Prov. 13:22. Wealth will transfer to God's Kingdom which will transform many in this season of harvest, glory, doors of opportunities opened and overflowing blessings of abundance.

God's people will begin to break loose from oppression, generational curses of poverty and having a poverty mindset. Many will experience debt freedom as they follow instructions (commands) in His Word.

Learn how to steward what God places into the hands of the faithful. God's economy is not a fearful, selfish way of doing things but a system that will give you freedom, liberty and peace.

As we are educated with the truth about money and God's intent for this tool it will take its proper place in our lives and be *used to bless us, bless others and advance the kingdom of God.* You will also learn there are spiritual gifts, instruments and tools that have more power to influence than money.

As we receive truth it is God's will we prosper and live abundant lives, it would be wise to repent for receiving lack and poverty which are curses. Instead, praise Him for the open portal of success in your life in every area. Remember, the Lord took poverty to the cross and gave us *His riches* (so we might become enriched with abundant supply, 2 Cor. 8:9).

The transfer of wealth goes beyond increase in finances and will include increase in favor, real estate, businesses, inventions, ideas and strategies released that will put His people in places of authority around the world, Deut. 8:18.

Also found in the transfer will be promotions, inheritances, physical healings manifested, restoration and reconciliation with families, an increase of singles marrying and the list goes on.

With the right perception of money, you will be able to handle it in a much more effective and godly way.

Appendices have been added to demonstrate and explain ways to successfully come out of debt, operate in God's economy and to maintain it.

In this resource discover how you can reap your harvest. In addition, recover what was stolen not only from you but from generations before you in your bloodline who planted seed and never saw the fullness of their harvest!

Realize you are not alone to manage funds entrusted to you. God is with you imparting wisdom and strength you may not have, but He does! Notice the following order: money, you and God. When we reject Him then the order becomes: money, you and the adversary. One or the other will be with you to assist you in managing your money. *You* will have to choose who it will be. However, be mindful no choice is a choice for the adversary.

Know God is returning for *a glorious church.* This season of harvest will help prepare His church to walk in their true identity which will encompass their purpose. Many will be promoted to leadership throughout the earth. As people begin to walk into their destiny it will require funds and the use of God's Economy.

They should also be educated with the knowledge of the One New Man, Eph. 2:14-20. The One New Man is comprised of Jew and Gentile in Messiah, Believers. (See *God's Way and Family, Chapter two* for additional information.) God's people are being trained and prepared to minister and train others to be ready for Jesus' return. One area of training will entail God's Economic System to know where to place their trust to have their needs met.

Why is this important? His people on earth in these Last Days are in the forefront by becoming His glorious church which He is coming back for. When the body of Christ experiences the Catching Away (rapture), those who are *not* ready (born-again; saved) will be left behind. Once the rapture occurs, those left, if they are not educated about God's Economy they may, out of fear and/or ignorance, take the mark of the Beast in order to have *power to buy or sell,* Revelation 13:16-18.

Those left behind should also have had prior knowledge of the anti-Christ and the beast to know not to take a mark [stamped] on their right hand or forehead to identify them as belonging to the kingdom of darkness in order to have power to buy or sell.

What is unknown to most is they will lose their identity of who they really are after giving over their *soul* to be destined to the Lake of Fire and torment in outer darkness for eternity, Revelation 20:10, 14-15. (See *The Tri-Tribulation Rapture of the Church* by Robert L. Dickey, PhD for additional information and revelation about the choices available for those left behind.)

If you are a child of God, a giver of firstfruits, a tither, a giver of offerings, a giver of alms (to the unfortunate), a giver of time and resources as well as striving to live upright to honor God, it is time for you to be in a state of expectancy, Eph. 3:20. Expecting suddenlies to occur at an accelerated pace that will launch you through the right doors at the right time to receive your promise and walk in prosperity for His glory!

Chapter 1

Biblical Economics Assures Financial Progress and Good Success

Being aligned properly to achieve financial soundness, success and increase will require Biblical Economics. It will have to be a major factor in order for a family, a single person, a business owner or employee, a corporation and whoever or whatever entity that functions with finances to become and remain successful in these End-Times.

Also, how a married couple manages their family's finances is extremely important because a great number of marriages dissolve as a direct result of unbiblical methods of management of the family's income(s). Marriage is a covenant that has within it a partnership *between a husband, a wife and God.* Marriage along with family are the foundation of society. The fact God is a part of the institution of marriage (which He created) is an indication marriage has spiritual aspects in its foundation because God is a Spirit, John 4:24.

Therefore, when families have major financial problems and issues such as lack or poverty, it can cause an increase in divorces, homelessness, oppression, division and isolation as well as affect the economy in the natural as well as the overall atmosphere. The attitudes of people in their given society begins to change. They will have an alternative to either be a people of hope and joy with a destiny or a people of hopelessness, division, fear and without a future.

The decision made is based heavily on whether or not these people know who they really are. Their identity must be clear to them in order to have the right attitude about life and the many turns and paths that present themselves. In other words, they will have to know who they are in Christ and the only way to know is to know Him. (See *God's Way and Knowing the King.)*

This leads us to the remedy and that is, God's ways must be first in all situations personal, professional, business or casual. In John 4:24 it tells us, "God is a Spirit (a spiritual Being) and those who worship Him must worship *Him* in spirit and in truth (reality)." Most do not realize obedience (following the instructions) is a form of worship that gives honor to God. We are all given a choice to do our part. When we give out of obedience it is a form of worship. Therefore, we worship with our finances (money) as well. This is a spiritual law not an Old Testament law, (See *Chapter Six* for additional information and revelation in this area).

When anything is out of order it cannot stand. The foundation is not strong. When God is not first with what He has blessed us to receive in the way of streams of income: education and the doors it opens, skills, talents, businesses or trades, then it is disrespectful, out of order, a sin and worse yet, it opens a door for the adversary to attack our finances. For example, a spiritual attack may come in many different forms. For example, doors become closed to employment or crisis after crisis begin to happen that chips away at your savings or you have been reduced to living month to month on an income that is not sufficient for the economy today.

When God is not first in everything that concerns life: our marriages, our homes, our businesses, our workplace as an employee, a student, even the way we vote others into public offices that do not know God, all of these areas have a consequence when we make bad choices by not doing what is morally right. The standard to know what is right or wrong is the Holy Bible not a person or a group's opinion.

When God is acknowledged and in His rightful position in your heart and in your everyday life experiences, His Promise and Blessing through Holy Spirit is released to help guide us, empower us, strengthen us and impart in general. We receive wisdom, guidance, good relationships, discipline to have healthy bodies, increase in finances, provision or contracts released, protection and so much more. We begin to align with God's will and not the adversary. For it is written, "The thief comes only in order to steal and kill and destroy..." John 10:10.

Therefore, *all that concerns marriage and everything else in our lives is also a concern for the*

True and Living God. When His wisdom and principles are applied to our finances they will assist tremendously in receiving divine wisdom necessary for the increase and management of our currency. To have both divine wisdom, favor and money is better than only having money. Your goal is not just to acquire wealth but to have financial freedom.

Ecclesiastes 7:11-12 says,

> Wisdom is as good as an inheritance, yes, more excellent it is for those [the living] who see the sun. For wisdom is a defense even as money is a defense, but the excellency of knowledge is that wisdom shields *and* preserves the life of him who has it.

When God blesses you it comes without sorrow, Isaiah 53:4, Proverbs 10:22. Furthermore, He desires to prosper you with the desires of your heart, Psalm 37:4. The Word of God says, "Let those who favor my righteous cause *and* have pleasure in my uprightness shout for joy and be glad and say continually, Let the Lord be magnified, Who takes pleasure in the prosperity of His servant," Psalms 35:27.

Therefore, while acquiring your finances you will want to also be free of any anxiety or worry regarding money issues. Having a *biblical financial plan* will help ensure you keep God first and follow instructions in the Bible for a successful plan of action in giving some, saving some and spending some.

Once a married couple or anyone has revelation *everything* belongs to God, they realize He has made them trustees of His possessions. They are His stewards, His partners who manage what He has entrusted to them, as they operate within His economic system. Luke 16:11 says, "Therefore, if you have not been faithful in the [cases of] unrighteous mammon (deceitful riches, money, possessions), who will entrust to you the true riches?" In other words, if you are unfaithful and not trustworthy with "worldly wealth" who will trust you with the true riches of heaven?

God does not want anyone, married, single, owner of a business and so forth to feel vulnerable when it comes to acquiring or distributing money that has been entrusted to them to manage. We must all remember, if we are in the family of God then we "are not of the world (worldly, belonging to the world), [just] as I am not of the world," John 17:16.

We are a people who are in covenant with the Most High God and have access to Holy Spirit, angelic forces, protection, provision, direction, and all that is necessary to fulfill our part knowing our help comes from above. Our covenant is more than a promise, it is a sealed and irrevocable agreement. It is sealed for all who are redeemed, born-again by the blood of His Son and it is binding and forever, Galatians 3:13-14; Psalm 89:34.

We must also be aware that the battle for our finances is a spiritual one. Satan hopes to destroy our blessings of abundant finances in the natural which would destroy our ability to produce and gain progress in the Kingdom of God which would ultimately give glory to Father God and better lives for everyone involved.

Therefore, whatever circumstance has presented itself before you, the Word of God says to fear not because "God shall supply all your need according to His riches in glory by Christ Jesus," Phil. 4:19 NKJV. God supplies all of our needs when we believe, have faith and trust Him to do so. God does what He does "according to His riches," not according to our resources, businesses, or even the economy.

So, look beyond your resources and see the glory of His riches and the fact He is willing to make you a steward over great portions of it. As it is written in God's unshakable word.

In addition, the adversary would like nothing better than to rob you of any faith you may have in God for a turnaround in your circumstances so much so to the point you become depressed and feel hopeless and are willing to give up. But the Word of God says, "And let us not lose heart *and* grow weary *and* faint in acting nobly *and* doing right, for in due time *and* at the appointed season we shall reap, if we do not loosen *and* relax our courage *and* faint" Galatians 6:9.

When we honor God with our worship in giving and being thankful for what He has done for us He blesses and increases. As we worship Him in giving and not because we want God do something, He sees our heart and motive, Ps. 50:7-23. Giving in faith whether the deed or act needed is already done or not also pleases Him.

In turn you will also receive wisdom for saving. Saving for unseen emergencies, investing, purchasing the right things in the right places and using cash instead of credit. And along with that God giving you favor with people regarding the items for you and your household, Exo. 3:21.

The Bible says in Proverbs 3:9 to, "Honor the Lord with your capital *and* sufficiency [from righteous labors] and with the firstfruits of all your income; So shall your storage places be filled with plenty..." When you give money where He instructs you to in order to be a blessing you are honoring God through your obedience.

Finances are given to assist widows, orphans and families, they are given to your local church and to larger ministries involved in international missions and rescue. Finances are also given to schools, orphanages, homes for the homeless, medical and dental care. As well as given for the upkeep and overhead of the local churches along with their leaders and staff who work diligently to do God's will in assisting the public.

I Corinthians 9:13-14 NIV Sheds Light on Salaries for Leaders and Staff

Don't you know that those who serve in the temple get their food from the temple, and those who serve at the altar share in what is offered on the altar? In the same way, the Lord has commanded that those who preach the gospel should receive their living from the gospel.

As mentioned above when you give finances according to His Word, it is a form of worshipping God because true worship involves obedience. *When you give money, you are giving a part of yourself because you earned it with your time, talents and gifts.* As you plant seed with your time and/or resources into the Kingdom of God these are all excellent investments that will yield a harvest when done with the right motive in your heart.

So, as you give you are honoring and worshipping the Lord as well as being a blessing to others as commanded (instructed) in His Word. "The reward of humility *and* the reverent *and* worshipful the fear of the Lord is riches and honor and life," Proverbs 22:4.

God Never Plans for Anyone to Fail

There are two types of success, "in life, there is good success and bad success. Bad success is the kind of success which robs you of time with your family, friends and church, and destroys your health and relationships. With good success, on the other hand, you see prosperity in every area of your life. God wants you to enjoy good success." [1]

His plan includes the fulfillment of your purpose and with that comes good success!

Joshua 1:8 Addresses the Good Success that is for You,

> This Book of the Law shall not depart out of your mouth, but you shall meditate (speak the Word of God) on it day and night, that you may observe and do according to all that is written in it. *For then you shall make your way prosperous, and then you shall deal wisely and have good success.* (Emphasis added.)

King Solomon, known for his wisdom and wealth said, "A prudent man foresees the difficulties ahead and prepares for them; the simpleton goes blindly on and suffers the consequences" Prov. 22:3 TLB.

God's Wisdom and Ways are not of Human Thinking, I Cor. 1:26-27 tells us,

> For [simply] consider your own call, brethren; not many [of you were considered to be] wise according to human estimates *and* standards, not many influential *and* powerful, not many of high *and* noble birth.

> [No] for God selected (deliberately chose) what in the world is foolish to put the wise to shame, and what the world calls weak to put the strong to shame.

God chose the foolish things of this world and anointed and empowered them to be wise, successful, strong and on top of the seven mountains or pillars of institutions that govern and shape society. People the "world" deems or considers foolish and weak are despised because they trusted and relied on God their Maker, Who knows all things, is all powerful and can be everywhere at once by His Spirit.

I Cor. 2:14 says,

> But the natural, nonspiritual man does not accept *or* welcome *or* admit into his heart the gifts *and* teachings *and*

revelations of the Spirit of God, for they are folly (meaningless nonsense) to him; and he is incapable of knowing them [of progressively recognizing, understanding, and becoming better acquainted with them] because they are spiritually discerned *and* estimated *and* appreciated.

There are also specific times and seasons God has set in the earth where man (mankind) could receive wholeness (Shalom) and enjoy a prosperous life. Some of those times are during the biblical Hebraic feasts. One feast in particular is Pentecost, in Hebrew it is known as Shavuot. This feast deals with provision in the natural as well as for your spirit man.

"This feast commemorates the ingathering of the wheat harvest (God's *physical* provision), the giving of the Torah, (God's provision of revelation, which took place at Mount Sinai at the time of Pentecost.) and the provision of the Holy Spirit in Acts 2." [2]

God provided for us in the natural by giving us revelation on how to release provision from our storehouse and how to receive blessings directly from God at His appointed time. In order to have and enjoy what the Lord has for us we will need to stay close to Him in fellowship, doing things His way and following His instructions both spiritually and those in the natural.

Joshua served God all of his life and towards the end of his life he said something that is a primary scripture in our home *"But as for me and my house, we will serve the Lord,"* Joshua 24:15; 31. When your family is on one accord loving and serving God together that is the greatest success your household could ever achieve.

God's good success leads one to His prosperity and not necessarily to what a culture dictates as success and prosperity based on that cultures *limited views* of what success really is.

Chapter 2

Prosperity is a Part of God's Kingdom

One way God honors us is to prosper us. Apostle John prayed, "Beloved, I pray that you may prosper in every way and [that your body] may keep well, even as [I know] your soul keeps well *and prospers*" 3 John 2. *God's prosperity encompasses the whole of mankind. His prosperity covers every part of our lives.* And He desires us to be in agreement with His heart for prosperity which includes multiplication and increase, Ps 35:27. Therefore, His concern for us includes and yet goes far beyond our finances.

He is concerned about our overall well-being, our health, our peace, our happiness, safety and the relationships in our lives. He desires we fulfill our purpose and the assignment He has given each of us will bring us into the abundant life and fulfillment of our purpose He intended for us.

We cannot do anything for God or ourselves for that matter without our health. Even though most are expecting financial wealth as promised to assist in fulfilling their call and purpose we must first look at our health. When God transferred wealth to the Israelites when they were about to leave bondage in Egypt, He also healed all that were sick who partook of the lamb. When He brings you into your Promise

Land He makes you whole. We need to keep that in mind and retain balance in our lives. Someone once said, "Your greatest wealth is your health!"

Merriam-Webster Dictionary defines prosperity as, "The Condition of being successful or thriving; especially: economic well-being."

The biblical definition of prosperity is much more in depth. It began at Creation when God first placed mankind (male and female) on the earth and told them to be fruitful, multiply and fill the earth...Genesis 1:27-28. God desired for them from the beginning in the Garden of Eden to multiply in every aspect of life. This would develop into a fruitful life of goodness, good things and wealth.

They were to have prosperity in every aspect known to mankind while advancing or gaining in everything desirable or good, Ps. 37:4. Thereby, giving God the glory. They in turn would carry His glory along with wisdom, knowledge and revelation to the rest of the world. This in turn would give glory to their Creator as His glory would be expressed through their lives on earth.

In addition, God's plan was whatever they gained and were successful at because of being in His presence it would increase, cover the entire world and be carried from one generation to the next.

To be physically, emotionally, spiritually and financially wealthy also defines true prosperity. To prosper is to advance forward in anything that is good, even those things you desire. To prosper also means you have successfully obtained your desire by meeting your goal set from your heart's desire, a vision or dream which originated from Father God as a portion of your inheritance or destiny.

Furthermore, you may experience success in your business, some enterprise, investment that is producing or other projects you are successfully progressing in. In addition, God will place people in the right place at the right time on your path to give you favor and are equipped to make sure you accomplish what you set out to do as you are led by Holy Spirit, Eph. 4:7.

God's Prosperity Includes Divine Wisdom

Because Christian Believers are anointed at the time of salvation they also have access to godly wisdom. The wisdom of God and revelation of God is located throughout the Bible and can be utilized in any area of your life, Proverbs 1:2-8. As you follow instructions in the Word of God this will lead to success. As you prepare to cross over and transition to cross over into your promise from the Lord, if you don't bow to opposition or give up on the way to the finish line (the end of your trial or test) you will successfully capture your promise.

As we seek God for wisdom in finances He will direct us to use our faith, gifts, talents and resources. He has imparted these to us to open up financial streams or avenues to increase our income knowing He is to remain first in our lives. That includes placing Him first in our finances with our giving. Giving out of respect for His Word and out of obedience allows Him to give us opportunities for increase. According to His Word, He will multiply back to you at the appointed times what you have given because you decided to trust Him. Luke 6:38 tells us, "for the measure you deal out [with the measure you use when you confer benefits on others] it will be measured back to you."

Proverbs 1:7 Declares Godly Wisdom is Key,

The reverent *and* worshipful fear of the Lord is the beginning *and* the principal *and* choice part of knowledge [its starting point and its essence]; but fools despise skillful *and* godly Wisdom, instruction, *and* discipline.

Palms 115:13-14 says, "He will bless those who reverently and worshipfully fear the Lord, both small and great. *May the Lord give you increase more and more, you and your children.*" The Word is speaking about a reverence (honor and respect) type of fear. As far as your children are concerned, He continues by saying, *"A good man leaves an inheritance [of moral stability and goodness] to his children's children..."* Prov. 13:22.

In other words, a good man (one who is righteous in Christ) will leave goodness which is the manifestation of the glory of God. Whatever God blessed him with, whether it was tangible, or wisdom, possibly a love and kind soul toward others or whatever he possessed that blessed others, it was enhanced not only to bless his children but his grandchildren as well.

It becomes a generational blessing which is handed down because of the person's salvation and receiving God's glory in their life. The Lord declares His ways are different and more successful. He says, "For My thoughts are not your thoughts, neither are your ways My ways, says the Lord. For as the heavens are higher than the earth, so are My ways higher than your ways and My thoughts than your thoughts," Isaiah 55:8-9.

Prosperity Encompasses "The Blessing"

It actually encompasses "The Blessing" which covers all aspects of a successful life spiritually and in the natural. From the very beginning when God made a covenant with Abram (God later changed his name to Abraham) God said He would bless him and *in him "will all the families and kindred of the earth be blessed [and by you they will bless themselves],"* Genesis 12:3. Abraham was a man of faith and faith pleases God, Hebrews 11:1, 3, 6, 8. All those that live by faith and are a part of the family of God, including those by adoption through Yeshua HaMashiach (Jesus the Messiah) are entitled to the blessing of Abraham – the Abrahamic Blessing.

This blessing consists of ***material blessings of land, money and goods for you and your family to live a good and abundant life while on the earth.***

As we walk in the blessings of Abraham and extend blessings to others, we demonstrate God's Kingdom. It demonstrates what kind of a King He is. "The Bible teaches that we are meant to walk in God's blessing. Living in poverty, sickness or infirmity is not biblical. When Christians fail to tap into God's blessing, His work on the earth is hindered. When they fail to prosper, the Church lacks the resources to carry out its mission. Being bound in infirmity makes them too weak to carry out their commission."[1]

"If we *do* what He says, then we will *receive* what He promised... Blessings come when we learn to obey His commands and walk in His ways... But in reality, blessing comes to those who align themselves with God's purposes and timing. Such are the keys to God's blessings: When we align our lives with the revelation of God, blessings begin to flow."[2]

When we have a Reverent Fear of the Lord we are Blessed, Ps. 128:1-2 says,

> BLESSED (Happy, fortunate, to be envied) is everyone who fears, reveres, *and* worships the Lord, who walks in His ways *and* lives according to His commandments. For you shall eat [the fruit] of the labor of your hands; happy (blessed, fortunate, enviable) shall you be, and it shall be well with you.

A blessed person may be described as a person who is fruitful, they multiply in having family, good relationships and material increase. They are crowned with glory and honor and made to have dominion over the works of God's hands and all things are under their feet, Ps. 8:6. They have blessings invoked upon them because of Who God is. He will cause His blessings to materialize in their present life with respect to all things and also in the life to come. The book of Proverbs 10:22, tells us, "The blessing of the Lord – it makes [truly] rich, and He adds no sorrow with it [neither does toiling increase it]."

The Lord shall command the blessing upon you in your storehouse (financially this would be where you accumulate your money, savings, investments, certificate of deposits and so forth) and in all you undertake. He will also bless you in the land He gives to you, Deut. 28:8.

The Word also says in Deut. 28:4 "Blessed shall be the fruit of your body and the fruit of your ground and the fruit of your beasts, the increase of your cattle and the young of your flock." In other words, what He directs you to and as you follow through and put your hands to it, He will bless it. He will bless you with good health, and on your property and in your business, He will bless and increase you.

Being spiritually blessed includes unmerited favor. Unmerited favor produces supernatural increase, promotion, restoration, honor, increased assets, real estate, greater victories in your life, recognition, prominence, preferential treatment, petitions granted, policies and rules changed and battles won you did not fight. With the blessing of God, you can also function in the anointing of multiplication.

Spiritual gifts will operate more frequently because the Lord can trust and bless you with them for spiritual growth not only for yourself but for others to witness and be able to grow as well, (Gen. 12:3; John 14:14-15; Est. 2:15; 5:2; Ps. 5:11-12; I Cor. 12:7-11 and Ro. 8:28).

Psalm 5:11-12 says this about the Blessing of the Lord,

> But let all those who take refuge *and* put their trust in You rejoice; let them ever sing *and* shout for joy, because You make a covering over them *and* defend them; let those also who love Your name be joyful in You *and* be in high spirits. For You, Lord, will bless the [uncompromisingly] righteous [him who is upright and in right standing with You]; as with a shield You will surround him with goodwill (pleasure and favor).

One of the spiritual gifts in I Cor. 12:7-11 is the gift of discernment which is a blessing to help the children of God. It will help you avoid deception and bring clear hearing from God. You will have the ability to discern and distinguish between true and false spirits (for example, people who may be lying to you, you will be able with the gift of discernment to see they are lying or not who or what they portray themselves to be). You will find He will also grant you the spirit of wisdom and revelation as you seek Him.

The Christian Believer inherits blessings through adoption (Ephesians 1:5) as they receive their salvation that was provided by the sacrifice Jesus the Messiah paid at Calvary. Because of Jesus

(Yeshua) we also inherited every spiritual blessing (Eph. 1:3) which includes spiritual authority in His name to resist evil that comes to rob us of the good successful and abundant life Jesus acquired for us, James 4:7. Many have realized it is a blessing to those who receive and a blessing for those who give and giving is one way to activate the blessing of God.

God chooses, desires and empowers His people to be blessed. One reason is they will be in a position to bless others. As they do He will continue to increase them, so they can continue to be blessed and reach out to others.

We Should Bless Those in Our Household According to Galatians 6:10,

> So then, as occasion *and* opportunity open up to us, let us do good [morally] to all people [not only being useful or profitable to them, but also doing what is for their spiritual good and advantage]. Be mindful to be a blessing, especially to those of the household of faith [those who belong to God's family with you, the believers].

Blessing the Widows and the Orphans is the Only Pure Religion in the Sight of God as found in James 1:27,

> External religious worship [religion as it is expressed in outward acts] that is pure and unblemished in the sight of God the Father is this: to visit *and* help *and* care for the orphans and widows in their affliction *and* need, and to keep oneself unspotted *and* uncontaminated from the world.

Blessed people are spoken well of but are also persecuted. Persecution is not sickness and poverty they are a curse. They are evil spirits or forces sent by the adversary (enemy) to attempt to destroy you. Persecuted is being betrayed, lied upon, isolated, called names, mocked and the like. The Word of God describes how a person who is blessed may be treated by the world (unbelievers) and even other Christians who do not understand the lifestyle of a truly faithful and blessed person and what they may encounter in their walk (journey) with God. Those that are truly blessed will experience some persecution which only confirms their position in the Kingdom of God.

A Blessed Person is Described in Luke 6:22-23,

> Blessed (happy -- with life-joy and satisfaction in God's favor and salvation, apart from your outward condition -- and to be envied) are you when people despise (hate) you, and when they exclude *and* excommunicate you [as disreputable] and revile *and* denounce you and defame *and* cast out *and* spurn your name as evil (wicked) on account of the Son of Man. Rejoice *and* be glad at such a time and exult *and* leap for joy, for behold, your reward is rich *and* great *and* strong *and* intense *and* abundant in heaven; for even so their forefathers treated the prophets.

A blessed person of God should be whole. The Hebrew word for wholeness is "Shalom" and in wholeness there is peace, provision, safety, favor, good relationships with family and friends, wellness in every area of your life with no lack; nothing broken and nothing missing. *These attributes also describe God's blessing and prosperity which is included in making you whole.* When we are whole things will turn for our good and function in our lives the way it should, according to the Word of God which is our standard.

Shalom starts with God's plan for your life.
In Jeremiah 29:11 we will find God's future for us,
"For I know the thoughts and plans that I have for
you, says the Lord, thoughts *and* plans for welfare
and peace and not for evil, to give you hope in your
final outcome."

**Ephesians 2:10 says God Prearranged and made
Ready for us the "Good Life,"**

> For we are God's [own] handiwork (His
> workmanship), recreated in Christ Jesus,
> [born anew] that we may do those good
> works God predestined (planned
> beforehand) for us [taking paths which
> He prepared ahead of time], that we
> should walk in them [living the good life
> which He prearranged and made ready
> for us to live].

The Priestly Blessing (Aaronic Blessing) is a
prayer specifically designed to bless. It is said today
in many Jewish homes especially on the Sabbath as
well as in some of the homes and churches of
Believers. It reads as follows "The Lord bless you
and watch, guard, *and* keep you; The Lord make His
face to shine upon *and* enlighten you and be
gracious (kind, merciful, and giving favor) to you;
The Lord lift up His [approving] countenance upon

you and give you peace (tranquility of heart and life continually)." Numbers 6:24-26, Shalom.

God's Plan Includes Financial Prosperity

God's plan for prosperity is different from the world's economic system. *God's plan includes gold, money, silver, great goods to possess but it does not necessarily start or stop there.* Prosperity, hope and well-being are in His house, along with His righteousness, for His mercy and loving-kindness endure forever, Psalm 136.

Zechariah 9:12 says,

> Return to the stronghold [of security and prosperity], you prisoners of hope; even today do I declare that I will restore double your former prosperity to you.

John 10:10 declares He came that we may have and enjoy life, and have it in abundance (to the full, till it overflows). *His financial plan is to bring us into His Shalom, His wholeness and completion.* His plan is to prosper us and not do us harm. This prosperous life will be the result of dedication to God in keeping Him first in our lives. Being committed will cause us to have a quality life with an ongoing progressive state of good success.

King David prayed, "Let the Lord be magnified, Who takes pleasure in the prosperity of His servant," Psalm 35:27. At the same time God sends instructions through Timothy to the rich so their riches endure forever.

In I Timothy 6:17-19 Instructions are Given to Help the Rich Stay Rich Forever,

> As for the rich in this world, charge them not to be proud *and* arrogant *and* contemptuous of others, nor to set their hopes on uncertain riches, but on God, Who richly *and* ceaselessly provides us with everything for [our] enjoyment.
>
> [Charge them] to do good, to be rich in good works, to be liberal *and* generous of heart, ready to share [with others],
>
> In this way laying up for themselves **[the riches that endure forever as]** a good foundation for the future, so that they may grasp that which is life indeed. (Emphasis added.)

The one thing is needed to walk in the prosperity the Lord has for us is to *believe He gave it to you* and it is a settled matter. When Father God sent His Only Son to die and redeem mankind that included everything that was stolen by the adversary. Prosperity was a part of the blessing that was stolen.

As a matter of fact, the Word of God says when Jesus/Yeshua went to the cross that is when, and only when, He became *poor* "...that though He was [so very] rich, yet for your sakes He became [so very] poor, in order that by His poverty you might become enriched (abundantly supplied)." The NKJV says "... He became poor, that you through His poverty might become rich" 2 Co. 8:9.

He said He would meet your needs according to His riches, Phil. 4:19, but He also said He "came that they may have *and* enjoy life, and have it in abundance (to the full, till it overflows)," John 10:10. I do not serve a God that lies. If you believe He is lying then you have Him, the True and Living God confused with the father of lies, John 8:44.

"Jesus was always conscious of abundance. His eyes were on the Kingdom of God where there is always abundance. God does not want you to be conscious of the lack in your natural circumstances. He does not want you to live by how much you earn or how much you have in the bank. He wants you to be conscious of the abundance of resources in His Kingdom; be conscious first of the abundance inside of you. Then, what is inside of you will become a reality on the outside." [2] Emphasis added.

Lord Delights in Making You Rich
According to Deut. 8:18,**

> "But you shall [earnestly] remember the Lord your God, for *it is He Who gives you power to get wealth,* that He may establish His covenant which He swore to your fathers, as it is this day."

He Commands the Blessing Upon You, Deuteronomy 28:1-14,

> v.8 ...The Lord shall command the blessing upon you in your storehouse and in all that you undertake. And He will bless you in the land which the Lord your God gives you...

Those Who Truly Worship Shall Not Want Nor Lack Any Beneficial Thing, Psalm 34: 9-10,

> O fear the Lord, you His saints [revere and worship Him]! For there is no want to those who truly revere and worship Him with godly fear. The young lions lack food and suffer hunger, but they who seek (inquire of and require) the Lord [by right of their need and on the authority of His Word], none of them shall lack any beneficial thing.

The Father will keep His word to our forefathers, Abraham, Isaac and Jacob because of the blood covenant He established through the line of King David and was ratified in the Blood of Jesus.

Covenant People God Made Rich

The Bible is full of covenant people God made rich and they remained so until their deaths and then their wealth was passed to their children and their children's children. He is always looking ahead beyond just their needs or mission and looking at future generations in that person's life. Furthermore, it says in Isaiah 61:9 "And their offspring shall be known among the nations and their descendants among the peoples. All who see them [in their prosperity] will recognize and acknowledge that they are the people whom the Lord has blessed."

God Spoke to Abram Regarding Blessings, Genesis 12:1-3 NIV,

The Lord had said to Abram, "Go from your Country, your people and your father's household to the land I will show you.

"I will make you into a great nation, and I will bless you; I will make your name great, and you will be a blessing.

I will bless those who bless you, and whoever curses you I will curse; and all peoples on earth will be blessed through you." (Emphasis added.)

Genesis 22:17-18 Further Confirms God Blessing Abraham and Blessing His Descendants through Abraham's Heir,

In blessing I will bless you and in multiplying I will multiply your descendants like the stars of the heavens and like the sand on the seashore. And your Seed (Heir) will possess the gate of His enemies, And in your Seed [Christ] shall all the nations of the earth be blessed *and* [by Him] bless themselves, because you have heard *and* obeyed My voice. (Also see Galatians 3:8-9.)

God made Abram extremely wealthy and He later changed his name to Abraham, making him a father of many nations, Gen. 17:5. The same passage above except starting at Gen. 12:2-3, what God spoke to Abram is also expressed in the Amplified Bible as follows, "And I will make of you a great nation, and I will bless you [with abundant increase of favors] and make your name famous and distinguished, and you will be blessed [dispensing good to others]. And I will bless those who bless you [who confer prosperity or happiness upon you] and curse him who curses or uses insolent language toward you; *in you will all the families and kindred of the earth be blessed [and by you they will bless themselves].*" *(Emphasis added.)*

Now "The Lord said to Abram, after Lot had left him, Lift up now your eyes and look from the place where you are, northward and southward and eastward and westward; For all the land which you see I will give to you and to your posterity forever," Genesis 13:14-15. God made Abram very rich. And God intended for Abram's succeeding generations of those in the family of God (both those of Jewish descent and those grafted in) to inherit property as well, Acts 7:5.

Others the Lord made rich were Abraham's seed, **Isaac** see Genesis 26:12-14 and in 24-25 it says, "And the Lord appeared to him the same night and said, I am the God of Abraham your father. Fear not, for I am with you and will favor you with blessings and multiply your descendants for the sake of My servant Abraham." Isaac inherited favor as well from the Lord and God made him wealthy in his own right. He continued to increase and increase until he became very wealthy and distinguished. He owned flocks, herds, and a great supply of servants.

Most of us know the story of Abraham's grandson **Joseph** who became the second most powerful and wealthiest man in Egypt, Genesis 41:39-44. Joseph was the son of Jacob and Jacob was one of Isaac's sons who also had favor on his life for prosperity. We see God's word continuing to flourish on the lives of Abraham's descendants. We realize Joseph's position and wealth did not happen overnight. He went through a period training and testing and ultimately reached the place God had shown him in a dream when he was a teen.

His story is proof dreams given by God will come true if we are on the right path and remain on that path trusting God and having a willing heart and an obedient spirit. This way God will be able to show us His goodness and we in turn will be able to eat the good of the land, Isaiah 1:19.

Then there was **Solomon** who was the richest man in the world then and still holds that record today. "The temple he built for the Lord was estimated at $87 billion and this does not include his personal wealth (according to a report by the Illinois Society of Architects in 1925)." [3] Solomon inquired of the Lord for wisdom and knowledge to go out and come in before God's people. He wanted to rule in the eyes of God and be pleasing to God as He took care of the people. So, God not only granted him wisdom but because he was not asking for riches or other favors for himself, God also granted Him wealth.

The Bible in 2 Chron. 1:11-12, says,

> God replied to Solomon, Because this was in your heart and you have not asked for riches, possessions, honor, *and* glory, or the life of your foes, or even for long life, but have asked wisdom and knowledge for yourself, that you may rule *and* judge My people over whom I have made you king, ***Wisdom and knowledge are granted you. And I will give you riches, possessions, honor, and glory*** such as none of the kings had before you, and none after you shall have their equal. (Emphasis added.)

Another person made rich by God was, Job. The Bible tells us the Lord blessed Job's life, Job 1:1-3. But in one physical day of destruction, trials and test, Job lost everything. He lost all ten of his children to death, he also lost all of his livestock, servants and his wealth, Job 1:6-19. Though, in all of this Job chose not to "sin by charging God with wrongdoing," Job 1:22 NIV.

In the meantime, between his loss and restoration as Job continued to trust God in the midst of his despair, he became a laughing stock to his friends and mocked by his wife. But as he continued he came into a deeper understanding and fellowship with Almighty God who hears his prayers and answers him.

To his friends and to the world it looked like foolishness, I Cor. 2:14. Yet, their god is from their own hands and power. The enemy has blinded them in their unbelief, 2 Cor. 4:4. But Job found that "secret place" and there he was assured it would be alright. It was because of his decision to trust God (have faith) and his ability through being in God's presence he was able to remain stable in the midst of all that had occurred, Psalms 91:1.

And when it was all said and done, and the trial was over those same friends needed Job to pray for them and out of obedience and being faithful he did and then he was totally restored before their very eyes, Job 42:7-10. God allowed them all to see He really walked with Job.

Because of Job's obedience and faithfulness to go through the storm and continue to believe and trust God, (never giving up on God) he was blessed in his latter days with more wealth than he had in the beginning. His new wealth included 14,000 sheep, 6,000 camels, 1,000 yoke of oxen and 1,000 donkeys, Job 42:12.

He was also blessed with a new family of seven sons and three daughters, Job 42:13. Job was even given an extension on his life and he lived 140 years *after* being restored so he could enjoy his new children from their births to their children to the fourth generation, Job 42:16. Those that are upright, in right standing and obedient to God, "...shall spend their days in prosperity and their years in pleasantness *and* joy," Job 36:7, 11.

Father God also empowered Jesus (Yeshua in Hebrew) and had wealth sent to him. It says in, Matthew 2:7-11 NLT that "...Herod called for a private meeting with the wise men... he told them, "Go to Bethlehem and search carefully for the child. And when you find Him, come back and tell me so that I can go and worship Him, too! After this interview the men went their way. And the star they had seen in the east guided them to Bethlehem. It went ahead of them and stopped over the place where the Child was.

When they saw the star, they were filled with joy! They entered the house and saw the young child with His mother, Mary, and they bowed down and worshipped Him. ***Then they opened their treasure chests and gave Him gifts of gold, frankincense, and myrrh.***" These men traveled in a caravan and what they brought was not a small portion but much to honor and worship the Child King.

However, Herod's motives were evil and he did not really want to worship the Child but to do harm so after the wise men found and presented their gifts to the Child, "When it was time to leave, they returned to their own country by another route, for God had warned them in a dream not to return to Herod," Matthew 2:12 NLT.

We cannot out give God! He restores, He builds, and He heals. He goes well beyond only blessing with financial security. He is capable and willing to make your life "whole" in every area with nothing broken and nothing missing but enjoying complete shalom!

You may think those are all Old Testament wealthy people and question, does God still bless and/or provide wealth for His people today? God never changes, "Jesus Christ is the same yesterday, today and forever," according to Hebrews 13:8 NKJV.

Therefore, those that are descendants of Abraham through the line of King David are given, "The Abrahamic Blessing" in addition to eternal life through their acquiring salvation. Furthermore, the covenant is sealed by the Blood of the Lamb Jesus/Yeshua, I Cor. 5:7. So, to answer the question, are blessings and wealth for today, the answer is yes, wealth is for today!

The Word of God makes it clear what God did for Abraham was for his descendants forever through an everlasting pledge by God. In Genesis 17:7 it says, "And I will establish My covenant between Me and you and your descendants after you through their generations for an everlasting, solemn pledge, to be a God to you and to your posterity after you." Galatians 3:16 is the New Testament version of this scripture. Also, in Galatians 3:28-29 it says, "There is [now no distinction] neither Jew nor Greek, there is neither slave nor free, there is not male and female; for you are all one in Christ Jesus. *And if you belong to Christ [are in Him Who is Abraham's Seed], then you are Abraham's offspring and [spiritual] heirs according to promise."*

The Bible says in 2 Corinthians 9:10 – God will "...increase the fruits of your righteousness [which manifests itself in active **goodness**...];" and in Proverbs 13:22 where it says, "A good man leaves an inheritance [of moral stability and **goodness**]..." in both of these verses the word *goodness is God* actually manifesting His goodness in a way you can experience it with your five senses: you can see it, smell it, taste it, hear it and touch it because it is tangible. A visible thing that shows the evidence of what God has promised and told you He would do. In other words, your proof has been revealed by the manifestation of His goodness.

How can you leave an inheritance to your children's children if you are supposed to be broke, busted and in lack all of your life? **God never said His children, the covenant people of God, had to live in lack or poor health to please Him.** That gives Him no glory and who would desire to serve a God like that?

Reaping the Harvest, Inheriting Your Promise of Prosperity

When does prosperity occur? When God brings us into the fullness and purpose of His plan for our lives. When the harvest is ready and we are prepared to receive it, Holy Spirit will begin to guide you in the direction you should go. Some will face the giants that have hindered them in the last season. The door that was closed will have angelic forces to make sure they go through this time because there has been a major shift and it is time. They will know they are ready because they will have the determination, new strength, wisdom and the favor of God to go through the door(s) they could not go through in the last season.

The Lord and Minister of the Harvest Has Spoken, Luke 10:2,

And He said to them, The harvest indeed is abundant [there is much ripe grain], but the farmhands are few. Pray therefore the Lord of the harvest to send out laborers into His harvest.

They will have the faith to follow God's instructions, trusting everything is in place and the old giants (lack, sickness, fear, any stronghold or demons) have lost their power over what rightfully belongs to them. As you step out by faith the right connections, provision and angelic assistance will be in position to assist you in moving forward. The Word of God says, "We walk by faith... not by sight *or* appearance," 2 Cor. 5:7. We also learn to call those things that be not as though they were, Romans 4:17.

Furthermore, as we exercise our faith, pray and ask God for directions, strategies, and instructions; if you receive a green light (sense it is time to move forward) go forth with a peace. If you do not have a peace but a check in your spirit (feel uncomfortable in your gut) stop and seek God for further instructions.

Another good point is to ask God for confirmation before stepping out especially when major changes are to occur in your life. If you feel you should stop and wait, then keep doing what you were doing until you receive an instruction that gives you peace. The reason I say this is because the adversary has been around a lot longer than you and is full of lies and tricks. He tries to disguise himself or his voice to lead you astray. Be alert to deception.

God instructed mankind from the beginning to plant seed (Gen. 2:15) and He (God) would take care of your seed and cause it to grow, Lev. 26:4-5; Lev. 26:10. The Lord said, "While the earth remains, seedtime and harvest...shall not cease," Gen. 8:22. However, at the time of harvest it becomes the person's responsibility to reap the harvest by faith, Ro. 4:11-16. The harvest that is ready for harvesting has to be harvested by him, Mark 4:26-29.

Believers have been taught how to give into the Kingdom of God through giving into their churches, to ministries online and by helping others but most have not learned how to reap for their giving. Most still give, give, give and wait, wait, wait until some give up and go back to functioning in the world's system. There is a waiting period.

God will show you from the start of your walk or journey with Him what He has instore for you. What He does not show you is the middle of the journey where things may not be familiar to you or of the norm. But by faith if you continue in Him you will see the promise at the appointed time. By faith the process is – believe it, act on it, before you see or receive it.

When you plant a seed, you must wait for it to be cultivated and grow before you see the results. The same holds true for Believers, when you plant your seed (giving into good ground where Holy Spirit is directing you give) the Lord is preparing the harvest from your seed. The right connections, emotional healing of your heart or a physical healing, pruning of old bad habits and associates in your life or other things may need to take place in your life before you are ready to receive what He has prepared for you.

That is why you never give up in the middle of a storm where things may seem hard or frustrating. But know by faith the Lord led you in a certain direction or possibly you got off track onto the wrong path in any event, *God is able to bring you through and out to total restoration if you choose to do things His way, in His timing and not quit.*

Most Believers have not been taught how to reap their harvest and end up sleeping (lack of awareness) during the time of harvest and miss it altogether. This has probably happened to most people, Proverbs 10:5. And you may wonder what happened to my seed? The Lord does not forget about the seeds that have been planted into His house.

Many Believers are constantly waiting for the "perfect" time to sow. Well we know the perfect time will hardly come Ecclesiastes 11:4. Giving is a decision that has to be made by the individual. If you want His blessings you will have to do it His way. One cannot reap if they have not sown. It is like going to a bank to make a withdrawal, you cannot withdraw what you have not deposited.

The question often comes up, why do many of the people who do not belong to the Kingdom of God live better than most Believers. First of all, they do not serve the God of Abraham, Isaac and Jacob. There is no covenant of blessing attached to what they do. Everything they do to make money is based on them alone and their hard work. They suffer loss too and have hard times as well but rely strictly on themselves to resolve them or another person who probably does not know as much as them.

So, since they have goods and money they feel they are alright. This is called self-righteousness, you play by your own rules and standard. But they really live a very dangerous life because tomorrow isn't promised especially to a non-Believer who can suffer mishap at any time and have to leave their goods to spend eternity in outer darkness.

Since they are already lost the adversary's job is easy and they are no threat to the kingdom of darkness. But their example of having things and money gives a false perception to the Believer who is faithful to tithe and give and still not see a reward or what was promised.

On the other hand, most Believers have a battle with finances. Part of the reason is the teaching in religious church denominations follow the opinions of men as opposed to churches who follow the written Word of God and are led by His Holy Spirit. You see it is the anointing (power of God) that makes the difference. Jesus (Yeshua) is the Anointed One and all those who are truly His are anointed as well.

Many Believers are taught, in dead church denominations, money is evil or it will cause them to go on a path of destruction. Yet they pray and ask

God for help with basic needs most of which will require the use of money the very thing they are afraid of. I doubt they are believing for a miracle since some do not believe healing, miracles, tongues or anything supernatural is for today. They suffer poverty and lack (some not physical poverty but a poverty mindset and unbelief about the true will of God for them and His resources).

Then there are Believers who are doing the right things, living up right, believing God by faith and planting seed with their firstfruits, tithes and offerings, helping others and yet still struggling financially. Listen, we all have the same enemy, the adversary, Satan, who hates people and anything the true God loves. However, the reason they are in lack or need is because we all live in a fallen world.

We all need a Savior and Lord. We all need angelic assistance and Holy Spirit to help lead and guide us. The difference is many are doing what is right and some even war in the spirit with spiritual warfare. Some will remain in this state, losing all hope and giving up or staying depressed as opposed to those who are still thriving and making ground. The difference is the perception and overall outlook.

One does not believe because of what they see with their physical eyes and the other choses to take Him at His Word and believes what He promised He is willing and able at the appointed time to deliver. We do what we can do in His strength and faith and

God will to do the rest. He will make sure we cross the finish line.

When we are subject to God's plan of prosperity, staying in His will and timing, following His instructions, He will heal our hearts, remove the reproach from the last season and prepare us to go through the door He has prepared for our abundant life. The abundance He has prepared in the natural will consist of ownership and that prepared in the spiritual will be such things as, mysteries revealed with fresh revelation, insight and spiritual gifts being in operation, I Cor. 12:7-11.

Insight of our true identity and why we are truly on the earth will be made clear as we begin to walk in our purpose. Insight of Who God is, and other vital information that will be necessary to gain and maintain the victory will be revealed.

Even though the harvest will be both natural and spiritual. In planting the natural harvest, it will have to depend on natural things such as rain, good weather, not to be attacked by insects or animals and so forth for its cultivating to achieve growth and produce at harvest time.

Whereas the spiritual harvest is not dependent on anything or anyone in the natural. The spiritual harvest will always be available because its relies and leans on God, trusting He will not fail and produce what is needed because He said He would meet our need. So, if the seed is planted and a drought takes place, but you exercise faith and look to the true Source that crop or increase still come forth in the midst of every negative circumstance. The Lord has no problem in giving a miracle (supernatural move on His part) when one is necessary. One example of the supernatural is found in Amos 9:13.

Therefore, by faith reap your harvest. Once you have done your part and planted your seed, now command your harvest to come to you. Your harvest is your seed multiplied back to you, 2 Cor. 9:10-11. Expect a hundredfold return and tell the enemy to take his hands off of your harvest.

Commission the angels to go and get it by saying the written word and not speaking fear or doubt. You are a tither and have rights and authority given to you by Your Lord and Savior who is the only One who paid the price for it. The Lord will continue to sustain you until the appointed day you see the manifestation. *Harvest time is here, enjoy the fruits of your labor!*

The Lord has provided all we need as it says in 2 Peter 1:3 NKJV, "as His divine power has given to us all things that *pertain* to life and godliness, through the knowledge of Him who called us by glory and virtue."

However, keep in mind some things prayed for are *given when the harvest is ready.* So, exactly how do we take what is ours at the appointed time when adversity is still all around us? *God has provided, promised and given but in order to apply what He has given we need to take action as we are led by Holy Spirit. We must apply ourselves with diligence to His promises, exercise our faith and when we receive instructions go forward with His plan by doing what He says.*

If we work with Holy Spirit, He will give us strategies, wisdom, protection, miracles and dispatch angels for that particular breakthrough to take back what was stolen by the enemy and to also receive the new thing God is doing in our lives.

2 Peter 1:5 Confirms we must Diligently Work with Holy Spirit,

> For this very reason, *adding your diligence [to the divine promises], employ every effort in exercising your faith* to develop virtue (excellence, resolution, Christian energy), and in [exercising] virtuc [develop] knowledge (intelligence). (Emphasis added.)

Do not allow others to dictate to you about your call, purpose, assignment or to tell you who you are (your identity in the Kingdom of God and who God called you to be). *God knows who He purposed you to be. It starts with knowing who you are in Christ.* This entails knowing Him and His will for your life. As a Believer, start by reading His Word, receive revelation of who He is as well as who you are called to be as a son or daughter. This also involves knowing who your enemy is and knowing you were given authority over him.

We will also need to understand giving into the Kingdom of God. When you build and take care of God's house, He will take care of yours. We plant seed in good ground with our firstfruits, tithes, offerings and alms. This is a priority because God should and has to be first in our life which includes our finances if you are to experience His prosperity and maintain it. (See *Chapter Six* for additional details regarding planting seed with our income and reaping a harvest.)

Another issue is many Believers miss God's timing because they don't understand or have not been shown how to flow with His timing. The Lord lives outside of time yet He placed people in time. He created a biblical calendar for us so we can move in sync with Him and keep the appointed times He chose to meet with us.

So being in God's perfect timing in the cycle of life will work together for positioning us to be at the right door of opportunities He has prepared. If you are not sure on how to get started order a Biblical Hebraic calendar as well as listen for God's timing through His apostles or prophets or other fivefold ministers that are familiar with flowing in His timing. The Lord will direct you as you spend time with Him in prayer.

Also, ask God for favor with Him and favor with people, Proverbs 3:4. Favor in many ways is better than money. It can even take you further in life. Furthermore, be watchful (alert), ask God to give you the gift of discernment (I Cor. 12:10) and wisdom when it comes to doing business of any kind God's way.

He gave us instructions on how to activate and release prosperity in our lives. One is to have pity on the poor because it lends to the Lord and that which you have given He (God) will repay you, Prov. 19:7. When we have compassion for others and move on it with a sincere heart God sees this as you are doing it for Him and He repays out of His riches, Matthew 25:40; Phil. 4:19.

What we do should be done with the right motive. God looks on the heart. True religion isn't practiced in very many churches or among Believers very much these days, James 1:27. But as we get back to the work of the Kingdom of God which goes beyond religion and is capable of changing the world we will find the anointing (the power of God) will flow and dreams, signs and wonders, true revelation and mysteries will be uncovered simply because we choose to do things God's way.

There are other things that activate prosperity that are found in the Word of God and they are mentioned throughout this resource. Throughout history those that dared to follow the Lord and not yield to the world's system were not in lack and quite prosperous according to God's definition of prosperity which is far better than the world's definition any day of the week.

There are numerous scriptures in the Word of God located in the Old Testament as well as the New Testament that support the fact God has always desired for His people, (His children) to prosper. He told us to choose life or death (Deut. 30:19) and if we chose life we would find God's prosperity.

Chapter 3

What the Bible Really Says About Money and the Transfer of Wealth

The Kingdom of God's economic system is designed to empower its followers to prosper in every area of their lives and includes finances. Therefore, wealth is a blessing from God. **Why would God want to bless people with money?** *God gives the "power to get wealth, that He may establish His covenant which He swore to your fathers..." Deuteronomy 8:18.* The covenant caused the people to be blessed, special and set apart.

Furthermore, as we are good stewards over what has been entrusted to us by God the wealth will also be used to advance the Kingdom of God with the good news of Christ (The Anointed One, The Messiah).

Mark 16:15 says,

> And He said to them, Go into all the world and preach *and* publish openly the good news (the Gospel) to every creature [of the whole human race].

As the gospel is preached, taught, published and demonstrated *it will bring in the End-Time harvest of souls.* He also gives money as a blessing for His people so they may in turn be a blessing to others. In addition, money is used in the market place for the exchange of goods and services as well as the ability to buy or sell.

This may be contrary to what most Christians and Non-Christians believe largely due to erroneous teaching. So, what does the Bible declare about money and its relationship with Believers? Furthermore, are Christian Believers living without the resources, riches and tools God intended (In Hebrew - purposed) for their lives? If so, how can this terrible wrong be corrected? The answer is to repent, for believing the lie of the enemy then renew your mind with the Word of God and change your perception on how you perceive money.

Money is for everyone and it was not designed only for those with a profession. This also applies to those with a trade, a skill, a business person, a homemaker, a farmer and for anyone who has a dream and dares to put money into action to fulfill God's purpose for their life.

God will meet covenant people where they are in life, prepare and train them in His will then empower those who are upright and in good standing with Him to be wealthy in every area of their lives. This includes wealth in good relationships, for their health, wealth of peace as well as regarding their finances.

Money has been *called* everything that represents evil and is designed to destroy your life. I have seen and heard of *some people with money* who have had tragic lives with poor health, poor relationships, with bad attitudes, are miserable and are just plain wicked. Some of them have committed suicide and have left their millions and billions behind.

On the other hand, I have heard of *some people living in poverty* who have had tragic lives with poor health, poor relationships, with bad attitudes, are miserable and are just plain wicked. Some of them have committed suicide and left their poverty-stricken lives behind and their families in debt.

So, what is the difference, if money is supposed to solve everyone's problems, why do we see some of the same sad stories in many of the lives of the rich that the poor possess? Could this be a spiritual problem more so than a natural one? Yes, it is a spiritual concern first. *If money is handled or managed out of order regardless of the person's social status they will have the same unfortunate outcome because they are battling with spiritual laws that govern how money is to be managed.* (See *Chapters Four and Seven* to review the worldly perception of money.)

God discusses money in His Word and identifies it as a tool. It is used to advance the Kingdom of God through our giving of firstfruits, tithes and offerings, Proverbs 3:9; Malachi 3:8-10. Also, to take care of our family's needs, wants, taxes, for goods and services and to fulfill desires of the heart placed there by God, I Tim. 5:8; Psalm 37:4; Matthew 17:24-27 NIV.

As we choose to love, bless and really care about another person's well-being (are they experiencing wholeness in their life?), we activate a spiritual law. One that will open doors for our protection, blessings, opportunities and so forth. How does this happen? Because we will have fulfilled an instruction from God, which by the way is the *second greatest commandment* He gave to mankind. When the second is fulfilled along with the first commandment every other command or instruction given by God is satisfied and fulfilled, Matthew 22:37-40.

The First and Second Greatest Commandments given by Jesus the Messiah in the New Covenant are Located in Matthew 22:37-40 and it says,

> And He replied to him, You shall love the Lord your God with all your heart and with all your soul and with all your mind (intellect).
>
> This is the great (most important, principal) and first commandment.

And a second is like it: You shall love your neighbor as [you do] yourself.

These two commandments sum up *and* upon them depend all the Law and the Prophets.

If we can do what he says even if someone has hurt us in the past, remember that God loved us even when we were not all that loveable ourselves. He tells us to love others as Christ loves us and sometimes that is required in a tangible way. Therefore, loving others in some cases will also involve using money, John 13:34; James 2:14-17; Philip. 2:3-4; I John 4:11, 19-21.

History and the Believer's Perspective About Money

During the Dark or Middle Ages there was an attack on the Church through a Roman Emperor named Constantine who wanted to destroy the Church and stop the people from becoming prosperous.

Up until that time the followers of Jesus prospered in joy, health, faith, peace, finances and so on. He came to bring an abundant lifestyle, one they may enjoy and have to the full, till it overflows, John 10:10. He and His disciples also ministered healing and deliverance which brought about wholeness.

There was an attempt to remove God out of everything, similar to what is happening in these Last Days 2 Tim. 3:19; Matt. 24:1-44. *But, God's Spirit is still here* and He does not have any plans to leave us nor forsake us to go anywhere else, Deut. 31:6; Hebrews 11:5 NKJV.

Constantine did a number of wicked things and one that comes to mind is the fact he changed the calendar the Followers of the Messiah kept. Constantine moved the dates on the calendar around 325 A.D. from the Biblical calendar aka the Hebraic calendar God set in place to the Gregorian calendar aka the Western calendar that starts with the month of January.

But the Word of God says, "It is not for you to know times or seasons which the Father has put in His own authority" Acts 1:7 NKJV. And in Daniel 2:21, it says, "He changes the times and the seasons; He removes kings and sets up kings. He gives wisdom to the wise and knowledge to those who have understanding!"

The dates were changed so the Followers of Messiah Jesus (which were primarily Jewish people at the time) would not be aware of the feasts dates Almighty God told His people to observe forever, Lev. 23; I Cor. 5:8. In other words, *Constantine was trying to block the way for God's people to prosper with "The Blessing"* which came through obedience (following the instructions from the Lord).

But in spite of all the efforts of the adversary the Hebraic Calendar Almighty God set in place still exists today. The Jewish people and true Christians who are a part of God's family by adoption and are aware, still use God's calendar out of respect and obedience in order to meet with God at His appointed feasts and times.

Isaiah 41:4 says,

> Who has prepared and done this, calling forth *and* guiding the destinies of the generations [of the nations] from the beginning? I, the Lord – the first [existing before history began] and with the last [an ever-present, unchanging God] – I am He.

Constantine further, made it a law no one could give their tithes. He also noticed how the people were blessed when they gave their firstfruits offerings at the beginning of each new month as they also received instructions and prophecies from God's prophets about the new month. In addition, they acknowledged God on His Feasts (appointed times for God to meet with mankind) especially during Passover (Pesach); Pentecost (Shavuot); and the Feast of Tabernacles (Sukkot). Trumpets (Rosh

HaShanah) and the Day of Atonement (Yom Kippur) are also very significant as they are a part of the fall feasts. When these feasts were acknowledged the windows of heaven were opened and blessings were released and much revelation was given Malachi 3:10.

The priests and leaders in the church were also told to take a vow of "poverty." Because the people were not permitted to give for so long it became a habit and an unwritten law. The bad habit or disobedience became the norm therefore future generations were not taught about this so they were not familiar with giving firstfruits, tithes and offerings to the church.

Subsequently many of the churches became poor and now that is what the world (the unsaved) as well as many saved people (Christian Believers) expect and believe is the norm or the correct thing for the church and those that are a part of it.

So, the thought of giving firstfruits or the tithes and offerings and having prosperity which includes wholeness that entails good health, peace of mind, good relationships, property, having an abundance of money and so forth seemed like something that was never meant for the church or the Kingdom of God's people.

Jesus said in John 10:10,

> The thief comes only in order to steal and kill and destroy. I came that they may have and enjoy life, and have it in abundance (to the full, till it overflows).

It was never God's will for families to live in poverty and/or lack. The blood covenant Believers have with God redeems us from the spirit of poverty because Jesus took poverty to the Cross along with sin and sickness. *To have been released from poverty by a great sacrifice then to choose it, is a slap in the face to the One Who paid the price to remove it from us.*

John prayed, "...that you may prosper in all things and be in health, just as your soul prospers" 3 John 2 NKJV. Many "religious" institutions teach it is wrong to have money based on scriptures that have been taken out of context, like the story of the rich young ruler Mark 10:17-27. Jesus was pointing out this man's true god had become his money and his possessions. That is why he could not part with his "things" to follow Christ like the others did, Mark 10:28; Matt. 19:27-29.

Furthermore, Jesus was asking him to give it up not because it was wrong to have money and nice things but so this young man could receive revelation of what was really important for his life. Once, that had occurred, it would have been restored to him in greater measure, Mark 10:29-30; Luke 18:28-30; Job 42:10-17.

Using scripture to confirm what Satan wants instead of what Jesus has declared as a part of our covenant with Him is wrong. Those things Jesus desired and came and died for us to have as a part of the abundant life is worth taking a stand for. This is especially true when there are so many biblical examples that are very clear and support what the Lord has done and has given to His people to bless them.

The Word of God reveals many God empowered to be wealthy. They remained rich until they died and then it was passed on as an inheritance for their descendants Prov. 13:22. Many Christians who struggle financially need to stop living in fear of success and with the fear of having money. That doctrine is a trap to keep you out of a place of prosperity God has chosen for you to dwell in so your life will be blessed and you will be in a position to bless others. Furthermore, it is designed to keep you bound so God does not receive the glory for the abundance in your life others see. (See *Chapter Two* for examples people God made rich.)

What Determines Whether Money is Good or Evil?

Whose hands the money falls into will determine whether it is used for good or for evil purposes. If it is in the hands of righteous people in Christ and they are taught according to the Word of God to give their firstfruits, tithes and offerings into the house of God then the money will be used for the expansion of the Kingdom of God.

As they give their firstfruits at the start of each Biblical/Hebraic month, and give their tithes and offerings, God will bless the rest of their income in that month. Blessings include protection, miracles, promotion, healing, and more. It involves more than only receiving money.

However, if money is in the hands of greedy, selfish and self-centered people doing things that are unlawful then it will be used for wicked evil purposes.

I Timothy 6:9-10 Does Not Say Money is Evil,

But **those who crave** to be rich fall into temptation and a snare and into many foolish (useless, godless) and hurtful desires that plunge men into ruin *and* destruction and miserable perishing.

For **the love of money is a root of all evils**; it is through **this craving** that some have been led astray *and* have wandered from the faith and pierced themselves through with many acute [mental] pangs. (Emphasis added.)

Money in and of its self is not good or evil. It is a tool. Again, if God is not a part of your life or if He is in it but does not have first place then something other than God's will, will take first place. In most cases since money is used practically every day to meet some sort of need and if given priority, it won't be long before it tries to take the place of Almighty God, which will be impossible.

Moving money out of its place as a tool or a device and giving money first place instead of God and His purposes, moves money into a position of an idol. A place that allows money to dictate and control your life. That is not God's will for your finances.

Hebrews 13: 5-6 says,

Let your character *or* moral disposition be free from love of money [including greed, avarice, lust, and craving for earthly possessions] and be satisfied with your present [circumstances and with what you have]; for He [God] Himself has said, I will not in any way fail you *nor* give you up *nor* leave you without support. [I will] not, [I will] not, [I will] not in any degree leave you helpless *nor forsake nor* let [you] down (relax My hold on you)! [Assuredly not!]

So we take comfort *and* are encouraged *and* confidently *and* boldly say, The Lord is my Helper; I will not be seized with alarm [I will not fear or dread or be terrified]. What can man do to me?

You must *choose* to guard yourself against the love of money. If you begin to love money above all else and ignore the command (instruction) from God to love Him with all your heart, all your soul, all your strength, all your mind and to love others as you love yourself, then you have been deceived, Luke 10:27; Matthew 22:37-39. You run the risk of living in fear, worry, fretting, reasoning, manipulating and strategizing in trying to put your plan together to achieve success and fulfillment.

God Never Told Us to Love Things but to Enjoy and Use Them

Money is a "thing" not a person, we control it, and we do not allow it to control us. However, if we give it first place in our lives because we *love* it so much we can fall into the traps of greed, pride and covetousness (start to wrongly desire the possessions of others). To help us guard against this we are to remember to seek God first and know if we do this His way all these "things" will be added to us. Furthermore, *if we exercise discipline we won't have to live in fear of greed, pride, guilt and covetousness destroying us.*

According to Jesus we are to Seek First the Kingdom of God, Matthew 6:33 it says,

> But seek (aim at and strive after) first of all His kingdom and His righteousness (His way of doing and being right), and then all these things taken together will be given you besides.

When you guard your heart, you are keeping it pure and your motives will remain pure before God. When your heart is *not* pure or what you are doing, even for the Kingdom of God, is done with the wrong motive it is not rewarded by God. For He looks on the heart of a person not like men who look at the person and their outward actions alone.

This Point is Addressed in I Samuel 16:7,

> But the Lord said to Samuel, Look not on his appearance or at the height of his

stature, for I have rejected him. For the Lord sees not as man sees; for man looks on the outward appearance, but the Lord looks on the heart.

Therefore, keep a check in this area of your life making sure your motive and heart are right before God regarding the use of money. ***Do not shun money that can be used for doing good.***

A Transfer of Wealth will be Experienced in Societies where Believers Dwell

The transfer of wealth is a transfer of power. It is attached to the glory of God which is being released in the Last Days to the Kingdom of God throughout the earth at a greater level than anyone has ever seen before. True power is in the blood of Jesus, the authority of His name and in addition, Holy Spirit is here as we need direction, instructions and help. Therefore, when we receive Holy Spirit's instructions and speak godly words in faith, angelic forces are instructed to move on our behalf.

The world trusts and settles for only that which they can see with their physical eyes and unfortunately that includes the almighty dollar. They deem money as their wealth and power alone but as most mature Christian Believers know, true power goes far beyond just possessing money.

God will transfer wealth from the unrighteous to the righteous in Christ at the appointed time within the season we are currently in Prov. 13:22. *One strong indication it has begun is a shaking takes place in the land and everything that is not of God will not stand.* This indicates God is in the midst of doing a work He has already declared in His Word.

Hebrews 12:27-29 NKJV says,

> Now this, "Yet once more," indicates the removal of those things that are being shaken, as of things that are made, that the things which cannot be shaken may remain. Therefore, since we are receiving a Kingdom which cannot be shaken, let us have grace, by which we may serve God acceptably with reverence and godly fear. For our God is a consuming fire.

Darkness will continue in the land and grow even worse, but the Kingdom of Light will shine as the people of God will live in God's true prosperity of having wholeness in every area of their lives which will include health, peace, good relationships, provision, safety and much more.

His people will inherit the ideas, strategies and inventions that will be needed to be sustained in this hour. They will have a stream of wisdom that will be needed for the times we are living in. God will transfer more than financial wealth, *He will transfer whatever it is going to take to make His people the head and not the tail, the lender and not the borrower,* Deut. 28:13 and Prov. 22:7.

Whereas with God, He said in Jeremiah 29:11, "For I know the thoughts and plans that I have for you, says the Lord, thoughts and plans for welfare and peace and not for evil, to give you hope in your final outcome." The New International Version (NIV) simply says, "...plans to give you hope and a future." God's plans for His people always includes grace (the ability to do things they could not do, have what they could not have before and to receive what they could not receive before).

The Kingdom of God's economic system empowers Believers to prosper. And when it does it is viewed as a negative thing to many Christians and non-Christians alike. A major reason is from centuries of false erroneous teachings concerning money and the Belicver/Christian. Negative teachings about money was taught in order to rob the Church in the Kingdom of God (the people of God also known as the Body of Christ) to strip them of power and authority which also follows abundance and prosperity.

Therefore, to make this point the instructions were shared earlier need to be re-emphasized. In the Kingdom of God, the people are instructed by the Word of God to give their firstfruits, tithes and offerings, to have savings, to give to ministries that have international outreaches that reach out to help people all over the world and to other types of ministries as directed by the Holy Spirit.

They are also *instructed through the Word of God to vote into office on every level people who will uphold the truths and morality in the Bible.* This will align you further with the will of God. In turn it will cause your money to work in your favor because you chose to align with God's will avoiding traps by doing things God's way.

We are asked to be good stewards over what we have already been entrusted with and God will give an increase. We are to remain righteous before the Lord so He can bless our children and our children's children.

Blessing our Children's Children, Proverbs 13:22,

A good man leaves an inheritance [of moral stability and goodness] to his children's children, and the wealth of the sinner [finds its way eventually] into the hands of the righteous, for whom it was laid up.

The Kingdom's Economic System, which is a higher system, teaches us to give, be fruitful and productive with our resources and finances and to bless others. In doing so we are following the ways of Christ Jesus our Messiah and at the same time giving glory to our heavenly Father, YHVH the Great I AM! Ex. 3:14.

This Brief Quote Defines Christian Economics, those in the Kingdom of God Who Incorporate God's Plan in their Finances and Everyday Living, [1]

Since economics is the science that deals with production, distribution, and consumption of goods and services, Christian Economics is the "discipline that studies the application of Biblical principles or laws to the production, distribution, and consumption of goods and services." It entails "how men use God-given natural resources, ideas, and energy to meet their human needs and glorify Him."

Christianity produces internal liberty in man, which is the foundation for a Christian economy. The internal change of heart that Christ brings produces Christian character and self-government which is necessary for an economy to be prosperous. Christian character and self-government: People who will not steal; People with a strong work ethic who will labor hard and be productive. This will cause an economy to grow; People who save and invest to acquire greater return later; and People who have concern for their posterity and will seek to pass on a greater estate than they received.

The truth of the gospel also imparts new ideas and creativity to man which assists him in increasing his material welfare. This occurs as man creates new and better tools. In addition, man gains the understanding that God has given him an abundance to rule the earth and if he seeks His supply, he will find it.

When we do things God's way He will prosper us and we will not have sorrows come with it that the world has, Isaiah 53:4. Also, this is seen in Proverbs 10:22, "The blessing of the Lord, it makes [truly] rich, and He adds no sorrow with it [neither does toiling increase it]." *We can increase God's way and keep our joy, peace, and have good relationships with our family and friends while we have rich and nice things.*

Why is this possible? Because our focus is not on the things because we realize they are only things to enjoy. We are called to love God and people. If we keep the correct perspective the "things" that are added as a part of the reward and blessing for making the decision to handle our finances the way God intended for them to be handled won't get out of balance and cause us to stray. "For the Kingdom of God is not meat and drink; but righteousness, and peace, and joy in the Holy Ghost" (Spirit), Romans 14:17 KJV.

We are instructed to seek His righteousness. Righteousness is "that state which makes a person acceptable to God." Righteousness is the force of absolute rightness; where integrity is expressed and is a part of your life because our righteousness is in Christ. We know that apart from Him we can do nothing except run the risk of being pulled off track by deception, John 15:5.

As long as there is peace the Holy Spirit is able to dwell and communicate with us. His joy gives us strength which is necessary as we trust God day by day. In Matthew 6:33 KJV says, *"But seek ye first the Kingdom of God, and His righteousness; and all these things shall be added unto you."* It goes on to say in Mt. 6:34, "So do not worry *or* be anxious about tomorrow, for tomorrow will have worries *and* anxieties of its own. Sufficient for each day is its own trouble." Instead remember, "But if God so clothes the grass of the field, which today is alive *and* green and tomorrow is tossed into the furnace, will He not much more surely clothe you, O you of little faith?" Matthew 6:30.

Receive the Gift of Wealth

The people of God are living in the most important time of all generations since the Day of Pentecost. As we approach the return of our Lord and Savior Christ Jesus, everything is pointing toward the specific event(s) which is known as the Catching Away of the Body of Christ. (See *The Tri-Tribulation Rapture of the Church* by Robert L. Dickey, PhD for more details.)

Before God's people (all those who have received the promise of Holy Spirit from the Father through His son Jesus/Yeshua) experience the Catching Away (rapture) there will be a massive transfer of wealth on the earth. This will not only include a great wealth of money, property, influence and resources transferred into the hands of Believers that has never been seen before, but it will include healing in every area of the Believer's life.

Healed physically, spiritually, emotionally, healed in relationships of all kinds from marriages to families, friendships, neighbors, co-workers and wherever there is a Believer who is a giver, walking upright and in faith.

God is the One who empowers a person to get wealth. Those people He empowers in that way know Him. If they don't know Him and belong to Him then what they have acquired in great wealth came through the world's economy and is controlled by Satan. In the beginning, the adversary, deceived

Adam (mankind, male and female) and Adam gave it to him, Genesis 3:6-7. Then Jesus came as the last Adam (Man) and took it all back!

Explains What One Man's Righteous Act Could Accomplish, Romans 5:18-19 NKJV,

> Therefore, as through one man's offense *judgment* came to all men, resulting in condemnation, even so through one Man's righteous act *the free gift came* to all men, resulting in justification of life. For as by one man's disobedience many were made sinners, so also by one Man's obedience many will be made righteous.

Satan stole it from God's people and transferred it to his own. Well, the time has arrived that *Almighty God is transferring it back to those in the Kingdom of God who are prepared to receive it.* It will come on the wings of His glory as His glory manifests greater and greater in this hour beginning in this season of harvest! Praise God for the supernatural transference of Wealth!

God is moving in the realm of the Believers financial prosperity for various and significant reasons. When the world's economy is shaken it is unstable, going up and down and sometimes to the extreme from one end to the other. The Believer, those that have learned to walk with the Word of

God, they will see favor as prosperity manifested in this hour as promised. It will occur during these End-Times and there will be such an overflow, one that has not been seen on the earth before.

What is transferring from the sinner (those who do not have a covenant with God) to the righteous (those who are in covenant with God) for? It is for the Gospel of Jesus Christ, the Anointed One to establish His covenant which God swore to your fathers, as it is this day, Deut. 8:18.

Many have held funds because of fear of loss or simply because they are hoarding their money and refuse to plant (give) into the Kingdom of God. They will in this new season receive their salvation and enter into the Kingdom of God with a heart to give and bless as God wills. And they will be blessed in return.

Those that will not cooperate with the Spirit of the Living God and choose to continue in their ways will find suddenly their ways will no longer work. Their money will begin to slip away from them. Leaving them in confusion as to why their methods and dealings no longer work for them.

Ecclesiastes 2:26 tells us,

> For to the person who pleases Him God
> gives wisdom and knowledge and joy;
> but to the sinner He gives the work of
> gathering and heaping up, that he may

give to one who pleases God. (Also see Prov. 13:22.)

Those who have little in the Kingdom of God as they continue to give they will watch the increase begin to manifest. The hundredfold return will cause money, property, goods and resources along with riches that were held back to now be seen. An explosion of wealth returned to the hands of the giver will be witnessed. Furthermore, the Kingdom of God will prosper and advance with The Gospel of Christ, The Messiah. Needless to say, things will burst open with new ideas, strategies, inventions, and favor as these things are birthed forth due to the wisdom of God's Word.

Chapter 4

God's Economy vs. the World's Economy

What most families and people in general do not realize is that there are two types of economic systems on the earth. One is the "World's Economic System" and the other is the Kingdom of God's Economic System (herein referred to as God's Economic System).

Both are a type of government, one has its own interest at heart while the other has the interest and well-being of all people. One is based on human wisdom and might, trying to meet its own needs, having a Greek mentality. While the other is based on the Hebraic biblical principles of God Who is the owner of all things, Colossians 2:8-10; I Cor. 2:14.

I Corinthians 3:18-20 says,

> Let no person deceive himself. If anyone among you supposes that he is wise in this age, let him become a fool [let him discard his worldly discernment and recognize himself as dull, stupid, and foolish, without true learning and scholarship], that he may become [really] wise. For this world's wisdom is foolishness (absurdity and stupidity) with

God, for it is written, He lays hold of the wise in their [own] craftiness. And again, The Lord knows the thoughts and reasonings of the [humanly] wise and recognizes how futile they are.

Comparing the World's Economic System with God's Economic System is an eye opener to say the least. God's ways and thoughts are much higher and greater than those of mortal men Isaiah 55:8-9. *When the World's Economic System is in decline God's Economic System, which is also of the Kingdom of Light is on the rise and will empower Believers to prosper.* It says in Prov. 13:22, "... the wealth of the sinner [finds its way eventually] into the hands of the righteous, for whom it was laid up."

Jesus came to fulfill the "Law" not to do away with it, Matthew 5:17. In fulfilling it He became the curse on the tree (the cross) so we do not have to endure the curse. Jesus did not change the order of blessing or do away with it (See chapter two for information regarding the blessing). What empowered a person to receive a blessing from God under the Old Testament will empower a person to receive a blessing today under the New Testament (New Covenant).

We are not excluding trials, test, tribulations, problems, attacks, broken hearts, betrayal, illness, captivity, lack, poverty, addictions, and so forth because some bad things will happen in everyone's life at some point if they live long enough. Terrible things may occur because we live in a fallen world. These and other evil devices are weapons that are formed against us but they don't have to prosper, Isaiah 54:17.

Furthermore, Jesus said in John 16:33, "… in Me you may have [perfect] peace *and* confidence. In the world you have tribulation *and* trials *and* distress *and* frustration; but be of good cheer [take courage; be confident, certain, undaunted]! For I have overcome the world. [I have deprived it of power to harm you and have conquered it of you.]"

However, how one handles attacks and how one receives the victory over them is what will make the difference. In regard to those who *only* acquire and/or accumulate money as oppose to those who have *God's prosperity (which includes God's favor and wholeness) and true wealth, supersedes only having money, they will take authority over the attacks and experience the fullness of life.*

God's Economic System is opposite from the World's Economic System because God's Economic System is managed with the wisdom of God and not mere intellect that does not offer the divine. God knows all things and is all powerful, therefore, we would rather place our trust in *a proven system* that has never failed than keep pouring into one that is *failing more* and more each and every day.

The World's Economic System basically comes from a Greek mindset. It teaches money is a god and it is better to store it up for yourself to increase and multiply your assets for you, your family and no more.

God's Economic System teaches us to store up as well but at the same time to give where He is asking us to give. By giving, the anointing (power of God) not only continues to flow but it causes multiplication. God's Economic system meets all of our needs even if something supernatural (a miracle) has to occur in order to make sure our needs are met.

As His sons and daughters, those mature Christians, trust the leading of Holy Spirit in regards to what He has entrusted to them to manage. They will not have to be concerned about money issues because they have learned to rest (trust) in Him. They will pray, cast their care and trust God for an answer. If their prayer was in His will it will manifest on time whether through favor or resources.

As we ask for wisdom and guidance He grants it to us. He "gives skillful *and* godly Wisdom, from His mouth come knowledge and understanding." The Word also says, "He hides away sound *and* godly Wisdom *and* stores it for the righteous (those who are upright and in right standing with Him)" Proverbs 2:6-7. **His knowledge is not the world's knowledge. His knowledge is divine revelation (full of mysteries) and understanding, Prov. 3:5-6.**

The Word of God says, "The reverent and worshipful fear of the Lord is the beginning and the principal and choice part of knowledge [its starting point and its essence]; but fools despise skillful and godly Wisdom, instruction, and discipline," Prov. 1:7.

God Delivered His People from the World's Economic System

The World's Economic System belongs to the kingdom of darkness. *It is not designed to prosper anyone. It is, however, designed to control and suppress.* The World's Economic System has fear, lack, a poverty mentality (in the mind and/or poverty in the natural), sickness and all types of bondages. It is a Babylonian type of worldly system God sent a Deliverer to set His captives free from.

In doing so God instructed a lamb without blemish be roasted and the blood from that lamb be placed on the door post and the lamb eaten and nothing of the meat remain Exo. 12:3-7, 10. God was breaking the world's curse off of His people His way and setting them free from bondage and establishing a new Kingdom for their lives.

All those who ate of the lamb that night, they were healed in every area of their life. The blood of the lamb that was placed on the door post and when the death spirit saw it, it had to *pass* over that house. *They were saved from destruction and they left that same night wealthy, healthy and free from bondage,* Ex. 12:8-14, 29, 35-36, 41.

As with the Israelites, which is our example, when God delivered them out of bondage from the World's System He empowered them that same night to have wealth and healing for all those who partook of the lamb.

Because of Jesus' Finished Work at the Cross where He became our Passover Lamb, God's Economic System was birthed into the earth, I Cor. 5:7. The Lamb of God was sent by Father God to be a Deliverer to set the captives free from bondage and that included debt, Isaiah 61:1-3.

Therefore, when Believers leave the World's Economic System and connect with God's Economic System they will be healed and empowered to get wealth, Ro. 8:17, I Peter 2:24, Deut. 8:18. They will be prosperous (3 John 2) and have liberty and freedom in Christ 2 Cor. 3:17 and Romans 6:14-18.

There is such liberty in Christ. To maintain a balance right-thinking people in places of authority and voted into office who agree with biblical principles, Romans 13:1-8. This will help ensure and preserve a just and righteous economy as well.

As we walk in our authority and we apply His blood by declaring it, it covers us so destructive assignments must pass over us and this includes destruction to our finances, Luke 10:19; Romans

5:9; 1 John 1:7; I Cor. 5:7-8; Matthew 28:18; John 6:63.

Church, Ministry Leaders and Staff Receive Compensation in Exchange for their Work and Service in the Kingdom of God

God's Kingdom does not operate as the world's system as we have seen. One reason is because His ways are higher than man's ways and so are His thoughts, Isaiah 55:8-9. Based on the Word of God and the Constitution of the United States is it true the House of God (the church) should *not* be taxed?

Ezra 7:23-24 tells us,

> Whatever is commanded by the God of heaven, let it be done diligently *and* honorably for the house of the God of heaven, lest His wrath be against the realm of the king and his sons.

> Also we notify you that as to any of the priests and Levites, singers, gatekeepers, temple servants, or other servants of this house of God, **it shall not be lawful to impose tribute, custom, or toll on them.** (Emphasis added.)

Therefore, it was drafted into the Constitution that the house of God would not pay taxes. To this day Churches are tax-exempt and under God's law and they are to remain this way for His purposes. Faith-based, Spirit-Filled organizations are set apart by God to be Holy and given provision to operate without interference from a government body.

According to the Bible leaders and workers in the church are to be paid by the Gospel for their services. So, when you give into God's house you are not giving to the people, the leadership or to those called to the fivefold ministry offices. You are obeying a commandment (instruction) to give into God's house *so there will be food (resources) in His house* Mal. 3:10.

Many people do not tithe nor give offerings because they feel they are supporting a minister's lifestyle. However, the Bible says, "...those who minister the holy things eat *of the things* of the temple, and those who serve at the altar partake of *the offerings...* that those who *preach the gospel should live from the gospel,"* I Cor. 9:13-14 NKJV.

Also, in Numbers 18:21 NKJV it says, ***"Behold, I have given the children of Levi all the tithes in Israel as an inheritance in return for the work*** which they perform, the work of the tabernacle of meeting." The Levites represent those who worked the altar and all the House of God.

The Tabernacle of Meeting was the house of God in the Old Covenant. In Num. 18:23 NKJV it says, "But the Levites shall perform the work of the tabernacle of meeting... *it shall be* a statute forever, throughout the generations..." *Throughout each generation the people who work in the House of God shall be compensated by the House of God.*

Ministers of the Gospel are Born-again individuals who are called by God to do a work for Him and they share in the same covenant by adoption into the family of God, Ephesians 1:3-5. In some locations the apostles chose and decided to devote themselves to prayer and the ministry of the Word and appoint others who were trustworthy to run the business to free them up for what God commissioned them to do. They had to set their priorities and exercise effective time management.

This would also apply in a home where the pastors or ministers of the fivefold (Eph. 4:11-12) would hire help to run the household or the church facility or the ministry so they would be freed up to spend the time they needed with God to receive fresh revelation and messages, instructions and strategies from God for His people, Acts 6:2-4).

In the book of I Thessalonians 2:9, it gives an example of those in the fivefold who were working on a second employment in addition to their work in the ministry. Apostle Paul states they chose in this case to work and preach the Gospel. By doing so it is allowed but the people may not receive the fullness of what God has to offer through these vessels because of the time they could not devote to fellowship with God and study.

But in all due respect a man or woman of God, as fivefold ministers, should understand they have a right to be compensated (paid) for their work in the ministry. In I Cor. 9:18 it explains this point, "What then is the [actual] reward that I get? Just this: that in my preaching the good news (the Gospel), I may offer it [absolutely] free of expense [to anybody], *not taking advantage of my rights and privileges [as a preacher] of the Gospel.*"

Therefore, it is wise on the part of the people to give and support their spiritual leaders if they want the fullness of what God is imparting to them in their time of prayer, study and growth. So the people attending a service will be full and blessed by an anointed vessel.

One other point regarding I Thess. 2:9 where other employment or streams of income is welcomed in addition to being called to minister to the people. A great awakening is coming to the church. In the End-Times, in the business marketplace you will begin to see more spiritual leaders owning businesses and not working for someone else at a second place of employment.

We are in a time where a mandate from God will usher into Believers lives opportunities, businesses, inventions and other streams of income. He is entrusting them to oversee real estate and goods for such a time as this as God is revealing and preparing His Kingdom to step up and into position. Because it is harvest and restoration time not only will the fivefold leaders have a priestly anointing but they will also have a kingly anointing as well (discussed in a later chapter).

In this season the transfer of wealth will take place so the people of God that are aligned with Him will experience a great transfer of wealth in all areas of their lives. To be able to function successfully, God will impart divine wisdom on how to manage their time in order to continue fellowshipping with Him and studying the Word and other resource tools.

In a case and times like these, God will send qualified assistants and whatever else is needed so the man or woman of God stays well equipped for the task, mission or assignment they are called to fulfill. All those who are obedient to plant seed into their vision as directed by Holy Spirit will be blessed and receive an impartation of the anointing that rests on the man or woman of God's life.

Furthermore, in the Bible it speaks of transportation being given to people of God for their use. In the book of Numbers 7:1-6 it speaks of oxen and wagons that were brought to the altar. "...The Lord said to Moses, accept the things from them, that they may be used in doing the service of the Tent of Meeting (the House of God) and *give them to the Levites,* to each man according to his service."

The instruction from the Lord was to give the transportation to the man of God. Today the illustration would be a leader receiving a vehicle or a jet plane to do the work of the ministry for the Lord. Just like everything else the mode of transportation has changed from the days when Jesus walked the earth. The church flows with the season and modern technology as well. They use electronics, computers, other devices, all types of transportation and so forth to utilize the best when working for the King of Glory Who provided it for their use in the Kingdom.

We serve a Mighty and wealthy God. The ministers who are sent out to do a work will be well provided for, Luke 10:3-9. Whether it is a spiritual thing or in the natural, one cannot give what one does not have themselves. He is the owner of all things. He is prepared to make you a steward over much if you decide to follow Him and keep His ways.

What Has Functioning in the World's Economy Taught Us?

Most people learn to diligently operate within the World's Economy and do not practice the financial principles of the Kingdom of God. Usually directly or indirectly they have made money their god. Greed (in love with money), selfishness (stingy), cheating, pride, lack of integrity and so on accompanies the world's way of thinking and doing things. As a matter of fact, taking advantage of others is seen in today's business world as operating with good business strategy or being savvy.

The World's Economic System is a system based in "fear of lack" and therefore teaches one how to hold their money (hoard it), keeping it even when others could be blessed with a little assistance. This system does teach you to save and invest, however, it is for your own interest and purposes only. Granted, some charities will benefit from receiving donations but for the one giving, most of the time, it is not from the heart with the right motives but only for a tax write-off of some sort and that is all the reward they will have.

Because giving or planting seed (with resources and money) which produces a harvest is not encouraged in the world's system your money will not have an opportunity to multiply according to God's system. By not being faithful or keeping your money in balance by, giving some, saving some and spending some, it can become a curse instead of a blessing.

Poverty is usually the result of being afraid to give and prosperity is usually the result from being free to give. There are more ways to be impoverished than having a lack of money and more ways to be wealthy than just having a lot of money.

Investing in the Stock Market requires a lot of research, primarily because the system is set up for you to gamble with your income or investment money. Therefore, proper research and brokers are necessary to avoid unnecessary risk as much as possible.

One reason it is considered high risk is because you could lose your principle as well as the interest. Loss can occur because of bad decisions or when the stock market collapses or crashes. A crash usually takes place every few years when a shaking occurs with the economy because the stock market is man-made. Whatever is not of God when the shaking begins it cannot stand, Hebrews 12:27.

God's Economic System Does Not Function in the Same Manner as the World

It is not designed to cause you to risk your hard-earned income that is meant for other things. But if you choose to invest in the stock market be well informed and not only relying on a broker to make major decisions with your finances. *Learn to trust God and inquire for His wisdom regarding money matters.* He will faithfully direct and warn you regarding the market when your motives are right before Him and you worship Him also with finances given into His Kingdom.

The world's system encourages gambling and playing the lottery, two vices with the purpose of gaining and increasing at others expense as well as accomplishing their "get rich scheme." Most corporations at one time did business with the people's best interest at heart but are now seeking ways to charge more for less product and quality of service. Business today is conducted with the lust of the eye, lies, broken promises and failure to follow through on items agreed upon.

Many businesses treat customers as if they are doing them a favor when they call their business to engage their services. Employees can benefit from this information because many of them do not have very good attitudes on the phone. They forget so easily that customer care is extremely important for a business and the fact that God loves people and desires that we speak and show respect to one another. Furthermore, some businesses over charge for basic goods and/or services by adding hidden charges and cost.

When you disrespect or come against people, especially godly people, and take advantage of them you are surely setting yourself up to have things taken from you. Galatians 6:7 says, "...For whatever a man sows, that *and* that only is what he will reap."

Government and State agencies are at an all-time high of exercising usury by over taxing and charging high interest and penalties, Luke 19:7-8; Neh.5:1-12; Ps. 15:5. Nowadays, it is the norm "to get over on someone else." In other words, it is seen as normal business practices to lie, not follow through, cheat, steal and exercise a total lack of integrity towards whomever you are doing business with. *These methods or practices are not a part of God's Economic System.*

Mistreating People and Setting Your Hope on Uncertain Riches, I Timothy 6:17-19,

> As for the rich in this world, charge them not to be proud and arrogant and contemptuous of others, nor to set their hopes on uncertain riches, but on God, Who richly and ceaselessly provides us with everything for [our] enjoyment.
>
> [Charge them] to do good, to be rich in good works, to be liberal *and* generous of heart, ready to share [with others], In this way laying up for themselves [the riches that endure forever as] a good foundation for the future, so that they may grasp that which is life indeed.

It is acceptable and taken for granted it is alright for people to place their trust in uncertain riches as well as for them to scheme and trick others. Since God declares He enables people to get wealth we are not against the rich or well to do people because all of them are not practicing these things or have evil ways. One can find bad practices and evil ways among the poor and middle class as well. *This message is for anyone who feels it is alright to take advantage of someone else.*

Many times, people act a certain way at their place of employment or business because the world's system does not offer much hope. The day in and out routine without motivation, appreciation or hope of a brighter future does not give people anything to look forward to and thus there is no fulfillment. Therefore, bad attitudes and practices toward the public could be the results.

A person who lays up riches for himself just to hoard more than likely will never give thanks to God or think of anyone they could bless. The Word of God addresses this type of behavior in Luke 12:19-21, "And I will say to my soul, Soul, you have many good things laid up, [enough] for many years. Take your ease; eat, drink, *and* enjoy yourself merrily. But God said to him, You fool! This very night they [the messengers of God] will demand your soul of you; and all the things that you prepared, whose will they be? So it is with the one who continues to lay up *and* hoard possessions for himself and is not rich [in his relation] to God [this is how he fares]."

Notice we are not simply talking about someone who has riches that is not the point, we are talking about the "attitude" some have who have riches and how empty many of their lives really are. Further, notice money by itself cannot fill any void in your life and give you wholeness and a wonderful outcome.

For an example, if you think it can just listen to past lottery winners. Find out how money changed their lifestyle overnight in the natural as most of them remained bankrupt in their heart (spirit) and soul (mind, will and emotions). And many were financially bankrupt within a few years. One reason being, they had no relationship with God or an understanding about God's finances and principles. So, with that open door, the adversary left many of them in a worse state with regrets, broken hearts and broken relationships.

Because of his or her selfishness, what was stored up will be given to the righteous, those who received Jesus are the righteousness of God, 2 Cor. 5:21. "A good man leaves an inheritance [of moral stability and goodness] to his children's children, and the wealth of the sinner [finds its way eventually] into the hands of the righteous, for whom it was laid up" Proverbs 13:22. **God believes in blessing with riches He does not believe in riches being our god and replacing Him.**

So, whoever does this because of the influences and training in the world's economy will eventually experience the transfer of their portion of wealth to someone who remembered to keep God first. Those who were honoring God with his or her capital, by blessing others, being thankful for their inheritance and remaining humble themselves.

Chapter 5

Recognizing and Overcoming a Poverty Spirit and Mindset

God is the owner of all and has placed all things under man's feet and has empowered His people to get wealth, Psalm 8:6; Deut. 8:18. The Bible also says it is our faith that pleases God and we have to "resist the devil [stand firm against him], and he will flee from you," James 4:7. This includes standing against evil demonic attacks that are sent by him to come against us, Hebrews 11:6; Romans 1:17.

The Word of God also teaches us the wealth of the sinner (someone who is *not* Born-again/Saved) finds its way eventually into the hands of the righteous (those who *are* Born-again/Saved) Prov. 13:22. *Acquiring wealth without God and not giving into His Kingdom is illegal and therefore what has been robbed has to be returned to its rightful owner*, Mal. 3:8; Prov. 6:31.

The world's people expect those who have a personal relationship with God through Jesus/Yeshua to be poor. But it was never God's plan for His people. However, the expectation Christians are supposed to be poor or just have enough to live and get by on, is a lie that received and has circulated throughout the world for centuries. **Poverty is not from God it is a demonic**

evil force and a curse. God is not glorified when His people live in poverty or lack.

People see Jesus as someone who is Holy and since He is seen as the "Christian's God and Role Model," the thought is, since Jesus was poor (which He was not) then poverty must be holy. To be holy means to be set apart and special for God's use and it has nothing to do with poverty. However, because the opposite conclusion is drawn, in order for a Christian to have wealth it is considered a sin, a trap or a theft of some sort.

This reasoning is completely false and not generated from anything or anyone that is truly holy. The real trap and sin, is for a Christian to believe and receive the lie and to settle for living in poverty not receiving the blessings and tools God intended for His people to have.

Needless to say, this goes against everything written from the book of Genesis to the book of Revelation. *To embrace poverty is one of the greatest falsehoods introduced to the Body of Christ/Messiah (Jesus' church).* It comes directly from the father of lies, John 8:44.

In addition, with *certain "religious" institutions and/or denominations taking a vow of poverty, this did not help the situation.* This religious mindset and practice began around the time the Early Church was experiencing heavy persecution which led to the Dark Ages when many Jewish people and Roman citizens who were followers of Messiah were being forced into this type of thinking. The early church or followers of Jesus/Yeshua were primarily Jewish people and the church operated with power seeing miracles, tremendous breakthroughs and growth. They carried an anointing which brought blessings, miracles and power to the people of God.

Taking a pledge of poverty brought a snare on the people and their families for four generations. This invited a poverty spirit and mindset to enter into the church. It was a trick and snare of the adversary. If you are improvised then you are not in position to help yourself or anyone else for that matter without it being a great sacrifice.

More so, if you lack understanding regarding God's will and reject the abundance which Yeshua came to give, you are refusing to allow God to prosper you, John 10:10. Prosperity is more than receiving wealth, it includes healing in areas of your life whether it is financial, spiritual, physical or emotional. So, you really shut a door when you believe poverty is a sign of spirituality when in fact it is a curse.

Jesus our Messiah did not come, die and rise from a grave in all power and authority for His people to live in lack and poverty. *That is not scriptural or spiritual.* **The Father's heart is to bless you in every area of your life!**

Therefore, there needs to be a renewing of the mind to heal the way people think about money,

Romans 12:2. A renewing of the mind involves people being re-educated about what the Bible really says about money so the curse of poverty can be broken, destroyed and overcome (See *Chapter Three*).

Jesus left a great abundance of wealth in heaven to come to earth. So, in comparison to what He had is what made Him *appear poor.* Even while on the earth He was not considered poor. Poverty was not a part of His life.

He did not become impoverished until He took our sins to the cross. *It was not until he took our poverty and gave us His wealth at the Cross on Calvary, did He really have any poverty associated with His life.* Remember poverty is a sin and a curse, He never sinned and He was a blessing not a curse, Deut. 28:1-14. He became those things in order to set us (the human race) free.

At the Cross Jesus' Actions Included Removing the Spirit of Poverty, Galatians 3:13-14,

> Christ purchased our freedom [redeeming us] from the curse (doom) of the Law [and its condemnation] by [Himself] becoming a curse for us, for it is written [in the Scriptures], Cursed is everyone who hangs on a tree (is crucified); To the end that through [their receiving Christ Jesus, the blessing

[promised] to Abraham might come upon the Gentiles, so that we through faith might [all] receive [the realization of] the promise of the [Holy] Spirit.

2 Corinthians 8:9 says,

"...though He was [so very] rich, yet for your sakes He became [so very] poor, in order that by His poverty you might become enriched (abundantly supplied) (See also John 10:10).

Jesus came to die and cancel our sin so that we might be rich in every area of our lives. His plan to take back the wealth and return it to whom He intended is already in motion. *However, "before the cross, Jesus was given great gifts of gold, frankincense and myrrh when he was a toddler in his home with His family*, Matthew 2:7-12.

When the disciples who were a combination of commercial fishermen, a doctor and a tax collector set aside their businesses to follow Him for a season and later preached the Gospel, these men nor their ministries ever lacked for anything.

Jesus' ministry also had a treasurer (Judas) something you do not need if there is no money. Jesus told His disciples not to take money with them on some of their trips so they could increase their faith and rely on God to take care of them one hundred percent. Jesus' clothes were so fine that the

Roman solders gambled over His garment," [1] (Emphasis added.)

Jesus was an extremely humble man but also straight to the point, Phil. 2:8-9. What He did not have in their travels He simply prayed and the wisdom was imparted along with signs and wonders to get the work done or whatever was needed to be fulfilled. They operated with natural means and spiritual wonders and lacked in nothing.

Unfortunately, in our society most people have learned to operate only in the natural with the world's economy and have worked towards what the world defines as success and prosperity and not what God says it is. The Bible speaks about the difference between the world and the godly. God is not of this world and neither are those that are in Christ, John 17:14-16; Eph. 2:6. Therefore, we need not be subject to the world's system.

Many Suffer Lack Using the World's Economic System

We have concluded people, Christians included, suffer lack for various reasons. In the natural on the surface it appears poor management of one's income as the main problem. But in reality, the lack and problem started in the spiritual realm first. Doors are opened to demonic strongholds when God's ways are ignored in the handling of money, Mal. 3:8-10; Prov. 3:9; 2 Cor. 9:8-11, Phil. 4:19; and Deut. 26:1-4.

A person or family may be dealing with a poverty mentality or mind set as the result of a poverty spirit that has been in their generational bloodline for decades or longer. *This makes it spiritual because you are in a battle with demonic forces who are on assignment to block your increase and rob the finances you have.*

For example, for a married couple and their family the world's system for managing finances amounts to a snare. Many families struggle financially for years until it becomes a major area that causes great stress and pressure to the point of separation and/or divorce.

More than half of dissolved marriages had an issue of how finances were managed in the home. There is either a lack of finances or miscommunication between the married couple, along with misunderstandings of what was meant to be of importance or not and the setting up of priorities for the use of their income.

It could be a problem because of a lack of faith, having separate accounts, lack of trust in their relationship, withholding tithes and offerings, not in agreement regarding managing of household income, over indulgence, loss of employment, loss of medical and dental benefits, high interest rates and inflation, having a poverty mentality (everything is for a rainy-day mindset), not enough money coming into the household in comparison of what is going out, and so on.

With this type of mindset, you are unable or unwilling to battle successfully. One reason being, you are unable or unwilling to see God for who He is and are unable or unwilling to fully trust and believe He will come through for you if you did it God's way. You are unable to wait on His timing.

Furthermore, you have a poverty conversation and confession such as, I can't afford this; we can't do that; it cost too much; I can't see myself living in that house or that neighborhood or having a vehicle like that; it is a waste of money to eat out on occasion; and so forth. ***When you speak in lack you reinforce the stronghold spirit of poverty that is working against you. You also prevent the power of God and angels from moving on your behalf.***

There are other spirits or behaviors that also contribute to poverty or struggling financially. Some of those have already been mentioned but may need to be mentioned again in order to group them altogether, and they are: the fear of lack which will prevent you from giving and as a result you withhold, firstfruits, tithes and offerings, the fear of success, doubt in God's ability or desire to help you, being prideful during times when you are prosperous, guilt and condemnation, sin and sin consciousness.

Furthermore, the spirit of Affliction may have been sent to devour a family, finances, your social life as well as your physical, mental and emotional health. The spirit of Pisgah tries to block your breakthrough; the spirit of Eglon (excessive taxation) is sent to rob you of finances; insecurity and allowing money to be your god of which both take you out of the realm of walking by faith and trusting God.

Also, laziness, procrastination, jealousy, envy, strife, heavy drinking, being wasteful, unthankful, selfishness, constant worry about money and things, seeking things first above God, bitterness, unforgiveness, impure motives, ignoring the laws of the land, plots and plans against others and not taking care of what has already been entrusted to you. *These hinderances block the anointing from flowing and bringing consistency of empowerment to bless you in your walk as well as to live with the blessings and promises of God.*

Many things have been attempted to resolve the financial problem in your life (higher education, trade schools, starting a business, a promotion at work, second and third jobs) but nothing really seems to work to change the situation. You are probably fighting unclean (evil) spirits that are working against the fruit of your labor and your harvest coming to fruition.

Resisting and Overcoming a Poverty Spirit and Mindset

Basically, the adversary desires for the Children of God to live in ruins. He wants their focus to be on the cares of this world, how we are going to eat, where we are going to live and what we are going to wear even though the Lord has asked us not to be concerned about those things, Matthew 6:24-25.

When your entire focus is on your personal and immediate needs instead of where it belongs, on your assignment and/or your purpose from God to bring glory to His name, to bless you, your household and others through you. You run the risk of growing weak and being overtaken by evil strongmen and demons on assignment to work against your finances.

You will not be in a position to fight against the kingdom of darkness and cause it any real damage if you stay in a weakened position. Ephesians 4:27 says, "Leave no [such] room or foothold for the devil [give no opportunity to him]." A change needs to take place but not just any change you devise on your own because as you have seen that does not guarantee any real change at all.

So, if you are dealing with generational curses of poverty affecting your finances the following instructions will help to set your finances free. It will remove the strongholds so your will regarding money will line up with the will of God and manifestation can take place at the appointed time.

How do we fight and break these generational curses regarding finances? The first step is to receive our salvation because the blood of Jesus that was shed will seal our covenant with God and break curses, Romans 10:9.

Next, we should receive the Infilling of the Holy Spirit with the evidence of praying in the Spirit (tongues) so we can successfully battle in the spirit without demonic agents knowing what we are praying about or what strategies God is revealing, Acts 2:2-4. (See *God's Way and Spiritual Warfare*.)

I Corinthians 2:4-5 says,

> And my language and my message were not set forth in persuasive (enticing and plausible) words of wisdom, but they were in demonstration of the [Holy] Spirit and power [a proof by the Spirit and power of God, operating on me and stirring in the minds of my hearers the most holy emotions and thus persuading them], So that your faith might not rest in the wisdom of men (human philosophy), but in the power of God.

I Corinthians 14:2 says,

> For one who speaks in an [unknown] tongue speaks not to men but to God, for no one understands *or* catches his meaning, because in the [Holy} Spirit he utters secret truths *and* hidden things [not obvious to the understanding].

These spirits will need to be dealt with in the spirit through prayer, repentance and decrees that place the right words in the atmosphere which has the power to defeat the enemy in a given situation and bring a turnaround for your good. Use the power of prayer and remain faithful to listen to your heart as God gives you instructions, strategies, wisdom and direction.

Also, use warfare prayers, praise and worship, and declarations to remove evil strongholds as you command and rebuke financial lack and generational curses of poverty to be removed and destroyed from your life. Then release the abundant life God intended for you to have, John 10:10. It will manifest at the appointed time if you are steadfast.

Now begin to put into action God's plan for your income (See *Chapter Six* the Biblical Financial Plan under "Married Couples Must be on One Accord in Agreement with Finances..." and see Appendix A).

In addition, learn of Him by the renewing of your mind according to the Word of God Romans 12:2. As you learn of Him begin to use the authority He has given us in His name. We realize we are not fighting against flesh and blood so we put on the whole armor of God to do battle, Eph. 6:10-18. We fight with the Word of God which "is quick, and powerful, and sharper than any two-edged sword, piercing even to the dividing asunder of soul and spirit, and of the joints and marrow, and is a discerner of the thoughts and intents of the heart," Hebrews 4:12 KJV.

We do not receive the reports that come from the World's Economic System declaring a recession or any other thing that is negative regarding finances. Those reports are for the unbelievers to instill fear and affect whatever little faith they have in any goodness or fairness in the laws of the land or the banking institutions. Christians are not under that economic system and therefore do not need to take heed (pay attention) to their reports and receiving them into their hearts.

When a shaking of the systems of this world takes place, whatever is not of God will fall. His people who are trusting in Him will remain standing and thriving, Hebrews 12:27-28 NKJV.

We walk by faith and not by sight and we will not be moved from our place of increase, 2 Cor. 5:7. We recognize we need to be in position as God is transferring the wealth to His Kingdom's Economic

System. We are to remember His ways so our "faith might not rest in the wisdom of men (human philosophy), but in the power of God," I Cor. 2:5; Prov. 13:22; Gal. 3:11; Hab. 2:4.

For example: I am subject to God and resist the enemy and all idolatry at the onset, James 4:7; Matt. 10:37. A thousand may fall at my side and ten thousand but it will not come near me, Ps. 91:7; Ps. 27 and Luke 10:19 which declares the Lord has given me authority and power to trample upon serpents and scorpions and over all the power the enemy possesses and nothing shall in any way harm me. And Psalm 113:7 declares, "He raises the poor from the dust and lifts the needy from the ash heap…"

Last but certainly not least know there is *a Name that is above every name* including the names of want, lack, poverty, past due, foreclosure, sickness and the like that will be removed from our lives once and for all as we conquer operating in the Kingdom's system to break and overcome generational and current curses.

The Name that is Above Every Name, Phil. 2:9-11,

> Therefore [because He stooped so low] God has highly exalted Him and has freely bestowed on Him the name that is above every name, That in (at) the name

of Jesus every knee should (must) bow, in heaven and on earth and under the earth, And every tongue [frankly and openly] confess *and* acknowledge that Jesus Christ is Lord, to the glory of God the Father.

As the Kingdom of God (Jew and Gentile in Messiah by adoption) progresses, the worldly sinner will be confused. The more they walk in confusion the more the Believer will walk in understanding. The Believer will be able to see clearly for their spiritual eyes will be opened in this hour so they can find their way and go through the doors God has opened and prepared for their call and purpose.

Your purpose is for the Kingdom of God. Worship and spend time with the Lord and He will reveal your purpose and confirm it through others as you are a blessing sharing your gifts, talents, acquired skills, anointing and ultimately walking in your assignment on this earth.

Remember, the wealth of the sinner or unbeliever (those without a covenant with God through salvation) is laid up for the just, Prov. 13:22. This word shall come to pass for all those who choose to renew their minds in faith and put the poverty mindset behind them.

As the transfer begins, slowly then will increase greatly in a way the world's people will notice their way of doing things do not work anymore and God's way is producing and causing His people to flourish. The World will watch as the places they once occupied in the seven mountains of society** have been transferred to God's Kingdom people.

In addition, we give thanks because of His sacrifice where He became very poor for our sakes. *"He laid aside His existence with the Father to be born for our salvation... giving up the riches of heaven, that we might be made rich with His blessings," 2 Cor. 8:9.[2]*

It is time to stop being a borrower and become a lender God's way, Prov. 22:7. Read on for instructions that will get you started in living the way God intended for you to live.

**The seven mountains of society consist of: marriage and family; faith/religion; education; government/law; business/economics; media/news; arts and entertainment.

Chapter 6

Removing Debt God's Way Using Spiritual and Natural Instruments

A godly plan of action is necessary in order to overcome the spiritual battle over your finances and be victorious in recovering from financial loss. *It is possible* for one to come out of debt by using spiritual and natural instruments and means. As Believers, we are asked by God to be good stewards (business managers with godly principles) over what we are entrusted with. This not only includes our home and family but it is for the single person, self-employed business owner and everyone that uses money. The same principles and instructions apply because the subject is the same, management of finances.

When God entrusts you with His wealth, resources of all kinds and value, goods and the souls of His people, He expects you to function with integrity, purity of heart, faith, humility, and character. The kind of character that operates or does business in an upright manner while maintaining your position of right standing with Him in every area of your life. He is not asking for perfection but excellence as a worshipper who follows through. This act of excellence includes our finances being in order.

In the midst of it all we realize money is only a tool and it is not our ultimate resource. Our Source is in Him and Him alone, Philippians 4:19. *So, when a portion of our income is applied to biblical truths and principles our seed (what we give) will resist the adversary and allow supernatural increase and abundance.*

Therefore, giving (planting seed) into the Kingdom of God, in good ground, is a part of God's plan for our income and the resources He has entrusted to us. This simply means, to give where God has placed His Name and directed you to for worship, there you will find the anointing (the presence and power of God). Deuteronomy 12:5 NIV confirms and tells us, "But you are to seek the place the LORD your God will choose from among all your tribes to put his Name there for his dwelling. To that place you must go."

At our local churches we are to fellowship with others, to agree as a body of people, to learn and receive the Word of God, to be strengthened by faith, to release and use our spiritual gifts and to meet others we can help and strengthen in return. The Word of God says that we should help one another as we *assemble together.*

Hebrews 10:24-25 Speaks to this Matter,

And let us consider *and* give attentive, continuous care to watching over one another, studying how we may stir up (stimulate and incite) to love *and* helpful deeds *and* noble activities, **Not forsaking *or* neglecting to assemble together [as believers]** as is the habit of some people, but admonishing (warning, urging, and encouraging) one another, and all the more faithfully as you see the day approaching. (Emphasis added.)

Therefore, as we cooperate with the Spirit of God, He can and does give an increase. When we are in right standing with God, He will enable us to bless our children and our children's children with an inheritance, Prov. 13:22. In addition, be in a position to help and bless others, Prov. 19:17; James 1:27.

As we move forward with God's plan to come out of debt one of the first things that must be done is to repent for being in debt. Then ask for forgiveness and receive the forgiveness and love of God. We ask for forgiveness because His Word says to, "keep out of debt *and* owe no man anything, except to love one another..." Romans 13:8.

Debt is a sin because the Word of God further tells us "...for whatever *is* not from faith is sin,"

Romans 14:23 NKJV. Many have fallen into this trap because of a lack of revelation, wisdom, information, faith, or because of a lack of discipline, generational curses or unfortunate circumstances of which some are from the adversary to cause failure.

Now that we are aware it is *not God's will for people to live in debt know He has a plan that will bring freedom from debt.* As we are diligent to follow His plan we will see the results we are expecting. Practicing these spiritual and prophetic actions will empower us to break free from debt.

By keeping God first and living upright in the power of Holy Spirit and doing the other spiritual things listed, it will cause the favor of God to be on our lives and that includes our finances. We are now in a position to receive favor for divine wisdom, strategies, resources and divine connections.

The favor of God also releases supernatural increase in opportunities, promotion, recognition, real estate, restoration and honor in the midst of our enemies. It will bring financial breakthroughs that will multiply back to us double for what we have been through (Isaiah 61:7) and give us a hundredfold return (Mark 10:30) not to mention the sevenfold the enemy has to return to us, Proverbs 6:31.

We call God's financial plan (budget) a *Biblical Financial Plan* (BFP). It is the instrument we used to get on track with God's financial plan for our lives and to maintain it. It is best to seek God first and receive in your heart the instructions to carry out the plan of action that is best suited for you and your family in order to set your records in order and remove debt from your lives.

The Master Strategist is Your Financial Planner

The Bible actually speaks about money more than any other subject. Seeking God through His Word by studying out scriptures that pertain to money issues will get you started. Also, adding Christian materials, listening to teachings from anointed ministers of the Gospel who teach on finances will also impart the wisdom of God to you in this area. The Master Strategist is the One Who knows all things and has created all for our enjoyment and use.

I Corinthians 2:5 says,

> So that your faith might not rest in the wisdom of men (human philosophy), but in the power of God.

Proverbs 21:30 says,

> There is no [human] wisdom or understanding or counsel [that can prevail] against the Lord.

In the Kingdom of God, the people are instructed through the Word of God to give their firstfruits, tithes and offerings, Proverbs 3:9; Mal. 3:8-12. They should have savings, give to their local church, give to ministries that have international outreaches that help people all over the world and to other types of ministries as directed by the Holy Spirit. They are to help others especially widows and orphans and to pay their taxes.

Natural Instruments and Storehouses to Manage Finances

Again, when any type of financial plan is not coupled with and applied to biblical principles along with divine wisdom it will usually lead to debt in one form or another. Before we discuss a biblical financial plan to handle our finances let us look at the instruments used in the "natural" by most people.

Natural instruments or storehouses used to manage finances may consist of the following: A checking and savings account, money market accounts, certificates of deposit, stocks and bonds, mutual funds, insurance plans, corporations and so forth. Any instrument used to store money and receive interest or a return.

Also, **if you are relying "only" on natural means or instruments** to increase your income and hopefully come out of debt then you may want to try worldly/secular natural solutions such as: working two and three jobs; opening a savings account to save so you can start paying off the smaller bills first. Acquire assets that increase in value with money you have saved such as CD's, mutual funds, or small pieces of real estate. Or you may try investing in stocks and bonds, foreign currency trade, in other businesses, filing bankruptcy and the like. If you own a business that is increasing use the funds wisely if possible and if it is decreasing try a new plan, advertise and so forth.

I believe most that have tried these solutions find they can be very draining and unsuccessful. Yielding no real results if you don't have the discipline to follow through with *"your"* plan as well as it taking months to years to accomplish them.

It takes time to build wealth especially using natural means, tools, strategies and instruments that offer no real assurance it will deliver as hoped or planned. We also understand there are risks and one must be prepared to take those risks.

Therefore, take your time and do the research and learn the best protection and type of entity; structure; tax strategy; the proper insurance for you and your family; learn about capital; how to best invest to protect your principle; record and keep good records; remove distractions and do not allow zeal to cause you to over extend yourself or make decisions too fast. And note, some things require a long-term approach or investment before seeing a return or the results you expect.

Also, keep in mind even though it is a natural instrument God can work through any device He chooses. When we keep Him first and acknowledge Him and ask, He will answer. For example, people of God invest in stocks and bonds the difference is, when they have a relationship with God He can and has told some to stop, take their money out because the Lord knew it is about to crash.

Managing Finances God's Way

A successful financial plan does not start with a financial plan or budget, a savings account nor building and investing in different properties, corporations or projects. **A successful financial plan begins in the spiritual realm first with your prayers** so you can receive divine wisdom, instructions and direction for your financial well-being and healing wherever needed in our finances.

If you have made a decision to do things God's way, you have opened yourself up to hear new and better ways of handling your finances with success. **When you incorporate spiritual dynamics, it starts with God's plan of prosperity that is tailor made for you when you are in the family of God.**

His instructions regarding your finances may come through His written Word, a dream, a vision or directly from the mouth of God in a still small voice. You may have carried this vision for years in your heart and suddenly have an unction to begin and step out and God sends a prophet across your path to confirm it all for you.

When working with God You will receive faith, strength, the gifts and skills He has allotted to you along with His connections to make it a reality and confirmation you are on the right path to financial success.

Deuteronomy 28:8 says,

> The Lord shall command the blessing upon you in your storehouse and in all that you undertake...

Today your storehouse would consist of any instrument used to store money and receive interest or a return. In the natural these entities may be used to store on earth what God transfers to you supernaturally. They consist of checking and savings accounts; certificate of deposits; mutual funds; insurance policies; money market accounts; stocks and bonds; gold; corporate investments

You will need to be sensitive to His leading so you can move forward in the right season with the right people in the correct location or with the right financial instruments (tools) required to bring what you endeavor to fruition.

You will also have an advantage operating with the Spirit of God, His Word and His host of angels at your disposal. These are resources to aid regarding finances the world just does not have. He will empower you with His grace to enable you to become wealthy in more areas than money. You will be blessed and live a blessed life as you follow the instructions in God's Word. You only have to *believe* and follow His instructions.

It will be necessary to maintain your personal relationship with Christ Jesus, the Anointed One, who will communicate with you giving you sound advice through Holy Spirit. In the book of John 10:4 and John 10:27 it says, "The sheep that are My own hear *and* are listening to My voice; and I know them, and they follow Me."

What exactly does this mean? Will I have to actually hear a voice in order to receive instructions regarding my finances? First of all, His sheep is another term for the Believer, those that are in the family of God. Secondly, the phrase "hear My voice" is referring to how you communicate with the Lord. When you pray or fellowship in conversation with Him, He hears you and will respond His way and in His timing. However He chooses to respond is considered by many as well as referred to as hearing God's voice.

How the Lord through Holy Spirit responds to you is unique and between you and Him. His personal relationship with you and how He communicates is different with each person. The way Holy Spirit responds on Jesus' behalf may be through a still small voice you hear in your spirit or through an audible voice only you can hear (on the average is very seldom, and for most, not at all). He may choose to answer you through His written Word as you read the Bible; He may answer through giving you a *peace* that goes beyond understanding; an unction to alert you or give you wisdom with sound advice for something you did not have a prior answer for.

He may speak through spirit-filled people which may include one of His prophets. He may speak through a vision, a dream or a circumstance or even a check in our spirit that will warn us if a wrong decision is about to be made. Or if it is a right decision at the right time.

However, the Lord chooses to respond we will need to be sensitive to Him as we learn how He is communicating with us. It may not always be the same way. You will need to discern (I Cor. 12:10) perceive or know with certainty what God communicating to you without hearing a voice.

You can ask for and receive confirmation on what was communicated to your spirit. There are different ways the Spirit of God will confirm what He has shown or spoken to you. He will also alert, strengthen and enable you to stay on track to have a good outcome.

God's way is to start with a plan that keeps His Kingdom first. As you take care of His house or business He will take care of yours. He will protect all that is entrusted to you.

Plant (give) your seed in good ground. Good ground for your tithe is where the Lord has sent you to be fed spiritually. Usually this is your local (home) church where you fellowship and learn of Him through His Word. If you do not have a home church, then sow into the ministry or ministries you are directed to by Holy Spirit that is feeding you spiritually and then give out of obedience. In some cases, the Lord may direct you to sow your tithe in more than one venue. Offerings are handled the same way, directed by Holy Spirit. Following through could cause a prosperous return on your harvest at the appointed time.

Before long with diligence and discipline you will be directed out of debt through natural means or supernatural miracles of the anointing of multiplication for increase or debt cancellation done on your behalf. The old will be behind you and new methods and strategies for managing your income will be in place.

Because of the renewing of your mind in the Word of God and having a heart for Him with the right attitude for managing your finances His way, hindrances will be removed and deliverance in your finances can take place at the appointed time, Romans 2:12.

Married Couples Should be on One Accord and in Agreement with Finances to Maintain a Strong Marriage

They should develop a biblical financial plan (BFP) together. One of them can be responsible for the actual hands on. Whichever one is better with details, has the time and understanding of how to work with a financial plan. Your spouse should be informed, stay informed and participate by giving their input to make sure all is running smoothly, making calls and helping with business, banking errands and whatever is necessary. (See *Appendix A* – Biblical Financial Plan.)

Both should have access to their biblical financial plan (herein afterwards referred to as BFP) but neither make any significant changes without discussing it first with their spouse. At the time of executing payments once a worksheet is written, both should review it and give their input and acknowledge whether they are in agreement or not. Keeping communication open about your finances and cooperating with each other will be a major factor in maintaining your marriage.

Are you both in agreement with who should have the final say about your household finances and how they will arrive at their decisions? Both should have input and come to a decision both can agree upon. Or simply allow the one more familiar with money matters to make the final decision. But if they cannot agree on who should be the primary person to maintain the records, pay the bills, follow-up on details and have more input and decision making then agree to allow the husband as head of the house to make the final decision.

Keep in mind, financial matters can be handled by either the husband or the wife. A wife is a helpmeet, he can defer or delegate things to his wife and it would not be out of God's order. That decision and how it comes about is between the couple. (See *God's Way and Marriage* for more details about a helpmeet, roles and husband and wife relations.)

If the husband decides to make a decision and his wife expresses that she is not in agreement with it and totally against what he is about to do and he does what he wants with their finances anyway, he has just opened a door to lose favor with God. Moreover, to cause bitterness and strife in their marriage and his prayers to be hindered and cut off.

I Peter 3:7 says Husbands Should Not Hinder or Risk Their Prayers Being Cut-off,

> In the same way you married men should live considerately with [your wives], with an intelligent recognition [of the marriage relation], honoring the woman as [physically] the weaker, but [realizing that you] are joint heirs of the grace (God's unmerited favor) of life, in order that your prayers may not be hindered *and* cut off. [Otherwise you cannot pray effectively.]

It is important to agree, to be on one accord and continue becoming one (like-minded) when married, Matthew 18:18; Phil. 2:2. You are *one* and in that there is strength to keep your marriage strong and in the will of God. If you cannot agree on a financial issue then discuss alternatives to accomplish your goal. If you still cannot agree then discuss it with someone whom you both trust and is knowledgeable about financial matters that can give input and ideas on how to resolve your present issue or long-term financial goals.

All bank accounts should be joint. This will lock the adversary out of this area of your finances where suspicion and mistrust can begin to grow. It will also allow both to use the same debit cards and checking and saving accounts. Once a transaction has been made the one keeping the detail records and recording on the registries for the various accounts should be promptly notified with receipts especially if purchases were not discussed beforehand (which is highly recommended especially for any large purchases).

As stated, both names should be on all bank accounts unless it is a business account (then it is optional) especially if one person is basically operating that business with the full knowledge and agreement of their spouse.

I strongly suggest each is informed before any purchases are made and agree on the amounts to be spent and the items to be purchased. This way both are held accountable to one another and both are informed about their joint accounts. If an accountant is hired to handle all of the paperwork and details year-round one of the spouses still has the responsibility to keep records and make sure all is well and things are being paid. Both should know what is transpiring with their accounts even though one does the recording and follow-up.

There should not be any secret accounts. Secret bank accounts used to save for an emergency marital separation will only help usher in the thing they fear. Hiding money and lying will cause a breakdown in trust and damage the marriage. Everything should be done upright and in the open.

Both should always know what obligations are on their BFP, what the due dates are and how the household income will be distributed to take care of it. Both salaries should be used for the household BFP with petty cash allotted to each for their personal use. Also decide on how debt that is brought into the marriage will be added to the current BFP and how will the old debts be managed and paid off. If filing bankruptcy is a consideration seek sound financial counseling first to make the best decisions that will fit your need.

Co-signing for relatives and friends should be discussed beforehand. It is not biblical to co-sign and place yourself in debt should the person you co-signed for decides not to pay on the debt for whatever reason, Proverbs 17:18; Proverbs 6:1-3; Proverbs 22:26; Gen. 43:9. The alternative to co-signing is found in Hebrews 7:22 where it tells us, "In keeping with [the oath's greater strength and force], Jesus has become the Guarantee of a better (stronger) agreement [a more excellent and more advantageous covenant]." In other words, trust Him for the correct way and to make it possible if what is needed is His will for their life or for yours if you are the one seeking someone to co-sign.

Where do you both stand with having a Prenuptial Agreement before marriage? With good intentions yet strictly worldly advice, ***at the onset of your marriage a Prenuptial Agreement would cause a major setback of trust.*** It also speaks to the fact you value your "stuff" more than your future marriage and relationship with the person you are entering into covenant with for life. It also programs your marriage to come to an end because you have already made plans for what you will take when it is over. *Biblically, we have what we say and what we truly believe, this is a spiritual law*, Mark 11:23-24.

So, if you make plans for your marriage to fail by planning to protect and keep what you worked for, then you will have what you say and believe. Don't be surprised if one day you find yourself, once again all alone with your *things.*

God caused a married couple to supernaturally become one on the day of their wedding after they spoke their vows to Him before witnesses. Now in the natural God requires they function as one. Their marriage is a covenant with God and He will do His part as the husband and wife work with Him to do theirs.

Other factors that are important for a married couple and the handling of their income are as follows:

- Before marriage they should discuss whether they will tithe and give offerings.

- Whether or not they both believe in saving and designating accounts for different goals.

- Whether having joint checking and savings accounts will be an issue.

- Do they both agree not to have secret accounts and be held accountable to one another, be open and up front about finances?

- Do they plan to make large purchases? For example, a house or luxury vehicles and if so, when in the course of their marriage? Do they plan to save and pay cash or make a large down payment or make a loan?

- What type of furniture is their heart's desire and how will they plan for these purchases cash or credit.

- Did the couple discuss before marriage and agree the wife will or will not work? This is very important to stop surprises later on, pressure on the biblical financial plan or blocking someone from their dreams and calling in life.

- Are they both comfortable with putting all their income together and distribute according to a biblical financial plan (BFP) that is set up and agreed upon by them both? (See *Appendix A* – Biblical Financial Plan.)

- How do they feel about recreational time and money added to the BFP for a movie and dinner out, travel, eating out with friends, giving tips, and buying things they desire if they can afford it?

- Are they both in agreement with who should have the final say about their household finances and how they arrived at that decision?

- What are their feelings or thoughts about money being set aside for themselves when they are older or if they are self-employed?

- What are their thoughts on helping an extended family member or friend acquire goods even to the point of co-signing?

- The couple should discuss their FICO scores and any debt issues before marriage to have an idea of what will be needed to set their finances in order once married. How they will manage the debt and what type of wedding they can have. Where they will live and how they will furnish their home if they do not already have these things to contribute.

- Have they discussed any payments to former wives and for children from a previous marriage? Payments to a former business partner? Or any debt that requires payments to continue once married.

- Does the couple believe in having a prenuptial agreement to safeguard what they bring to the marriage? If so, that is a great mistake.

- How did their parents manage their finances?

- Do they have any financial goals they have set for themselves?

Making a Withdrawal from Your Heavenly Account

- **Making a withdrawal from your heavenly account (spiritual storehouse) in heaven.** Once you pray over and release your firstfruits, tithe and offerings there is a corresponding deposit into your heavenly account. This is the spiritual part of planting seed (giving) into God's house. That deposit is multiplied so when you make a withdrawal it is always given back to you in greater measure, "And [God] Who provides seed for the sower and bread for eating *will also provide and multiply your [resources for] sowing and increase the fruits of your righteousness... "* 2 Cor. 9-10.

- **When withdrawing from your heavenly account be specific about the amount requested.** Lay hold of it by faith, Mark 11:24; come in agreement with another Believer, Matt. 18:19; use your authority in Jesus' name, Matthew 28:18; John 6:63 and bind the devil and his forces by standing on

Mark 16:17; Luke 10:19 and then tell him not to come back in that area of your life Mark 9:25. Now loose the forces of heaven, "whatever I forbid and declare to be improper and unlawful on earth must be what is already forbidden in heaven, and whatever I permit and declare proper and lawful on earth must be what is already permitted in heaven" Matt. 18:18; now send the angels to get what it is you are requesting that is in God's will. Thank God by praising Him for the manifestation. We serve a "now" God, Ps 118:25. Trust Him and praise Him for it being done even though you have not seen it yet. (See *Appendix B* – Withdrawal from My Heavenly Account.)

- **It could be returned in money, opportunities, healing, a breakthrough, or open doors that had been shut to you** or whatever your need is. By faith you plant something, now God has something in His hands from you He can work with. The disciples placed two fish and five loaves in Jesus' hands and He fed five thousand men plus thousands more with women and children, Matthew 14:17-21. That same anointing of multiplication will be on your seed when it is manifested, because you gave and placed it in the care of a Living God and it was deposited it into your heavenly account. When it comes back it will come to you in areas you really need a breakthrough or possibly a miracle.

Key Points for Removing Debt and Managing God's Way

- **Seeking God first,** believing and trusting Him by doing things His way will allow the anointing of Holy Spirit to flow in your life daily to guide, bring comfort, empowerment, teach you, instruct you in all your ways for your good in all that you endeavor, bring you into all Truth, to bring things to your remembrance and much more, John 16:7, 13.

- **Giving is a major connection that releases God's plan, "The Blessing."** It was placed on the earth for mankind to enjoy all the way back to the beginning of time and creation. Giving started before the Old Testament "Law" and it is for today because *it is a part of God's plan of prosperity,* 2 Cor. 9:6-11 and I Cor. 3:6-11. An example was when Abram was blessed by Melchizedek when Abram gave the tithe (the 10th) to Him, Gen. 14:18-20. You only rob yourself of the blessing it brings when you *reason with your mind* that tithing and giving offerings is outdated or not intended for the church when the Bible and much evidence says otherwise. (See *Chapter Two* for additional information regarding the Blessing.)

- **Consistently giving (planting seed) our firstfruits, tithes and offerings** is an avenue to prosperity. Keeping God first (Matthew 6:33) and living upright (striving to do the right thing) before Him will cause the favor of God to manifest in your life and on your finances. It will protect your finances as a part of your hedge of protection, Malachi 3:11 which says, "And I will rebuke the devourer [insects and plagues] for your sakes and he shall not destroy the fruits of your ground, neither shall your vine drop its fruit before the time in the field, says the Lord of hosts."

- **We are to give (plant our seed) firstfruits, tithes and offerings into good ground.** Good ground for your tithe is where the Lord has sent you to be fed spiritually. Usually this is your local (home) church where you fellowship and learn of God through His Word. If you do not have a home church, then sow into the ministry you are directed to by the Holy Spirit that is feeding you spiritually and then give out of obedience. In some cases, the Lord may direct you to sow your tithe in more than one venue. Offerings are handled the same way, directed by Holy Spirit. Following through could cause a prosperous return on your harvest at the appointed time. This may also include giving offerings to international ministries with outreaches that help people around the world with basic needs of drinking water, food, clothing, nutritional, medical and dental care, housing and educational needs.

- **Giving a Firstfruits Offering at the beginning of each new biblical month *is* for today.** We show honor, praise and thanksgiving to God for what He has done in the previous month as well as recognizing a new biblical month has begun. *Each new month is called the Head of the Month. In Hebrew it is called Rosh Chodesh.* Many are not aware of the fact the Lord has His own calendar mankind should observe to this day. He does not live in time, but He placed mankind in time from the beginning of creation when He gave us His calendar through His creation. For instance, day and night (one day, Gen. 1:5) the Sabbath on the seventh day (a week, Gen. 2:2; Heb. 4:9-10). And in Gen. 1:16 God established the sign in the heavens for a month when He arranged the moon to go through a complete cycle around the earth twelve times which by the way gave us a year. As we honor God by acknowledging the new month with a *firstfruits offering, it sanctifies (makes holy) the rest of your income for the month.* Romans 11:16 NIV says, "If the part of the dough offered as firstfruits is holy, then the whole batch is holy; if the root is holy, so are the branches" And in Proverbs 3:9 it states, "Honor the Lord with your capital *and* sufficiency [from righteous labors] and with firstfruits of all your income." (See *Appendix C* for additional information regarding Firstfruits.)

- **Feasts Offerings are also given at God's three main appointed times** during the year. The times God chose to meet with His people. The Jewish people restored the feasts now the feasts are being restored to the church. Keeping these set appointments will honor God and show gratitude. Honoring and recognizing Him is a major factor for the windows of heaven opening where blessings, revelation, fulfillment of promises and so much more are poured out, Malachi 3:10. These feasts are: The Feast of Passover; the Feast of Pentecost; and the Feast of Tabernacles. As a Believer (Jew or non-Jew) when you celebrate or acknowledge these feasts blessings are released. Nine blessings at

Passover; power at Pentecost for those blessings released at Passover and the harvest at Tabernacles. One of the benefits of being a One New Man (Jew and Gentile in Christ Messiah) is it restores the financial blessings of Kingdom finances into your life as a Believer. (See *Appendix D* regarding God's Feasts.) Also, the Feast of Trumpets (Rosh Hashanah) is a time to be aware of, for it is the beginning of the Biblical Civil New Year as Passover (Pesach in Hebrew) is the beginning of the Biblical Spiritual New Year, Lev. 23:2; Exo.23:14, 16.

- **Christians in the Early Church celebrated the three appointed Feasts** before the feasts were removed from the church when the calendar was changed and great persecution came against the church by the Roman Emperor Constantine around 325 A.D. Now in these Last Days during the End-Times, God is awakening the minds of His people and opening their spiritual eyes, giving revelation as well as restoration of those things, which were stolen from His church. Also, celebrating the feasts alerts us and makes us aware of God's timing. This is key, because to be in His will and timing assures you to receive what He has for you and your purpose in life. (Please see *Appendix D* for information regarding God's Feasts and whether or not Believers are to Celebrate them today.)

- **Beautiful Biblical Hebraic Calendars** will help you become familiar with God's appointed times and information regarding His Feasts are available for those who are led to honor God on His appointed days. To purchase a calendar please visit the online store of the Elijah List at www.elijahshopper.com.

- **Giving the tithe honors God and includes him in your finances.** We can appreciate money, learn its real purpose and use it as an effective tool. In addition, God will give the wisdom and knowledge necessary in distributing funds. When we choose to do things God's way according to His plan and will in all areas of our lives we are choosing to honor and give respect to God. The Lord is there to assist us whether we understand how much we need Him or not. When we tithe the Lord will give us wisdom and blessings, will cause our finances to go farther as well as give strategies and revelation of how to manage and increase it. Planting seed (giving) into the Kingdom of God first, sets the course for favor, blessings, opportunities, peace of mind, prosperity, real estate, good relationships, understanding and much more. If you are a ministry and you receive tithes from donations, giving a tenth of that tithe to other ministries is pleasing to God and is considered a tithe from your ministry to Him. It also blesses the ones who donated to your ministry, Numbers 18:26.

- **What is the tithe?** The tithe is Holy (set apart and special) and it belongs to God to maintain finances for His Kingdom (His governmental work of righteousness, peace and joy in Holy Spirit for His people, Mt. 6:33). The word tithe means "tenth." Malachi 3:10 teaches the windows of heaven will open and release a blessing. The tithe is ten percent (10%) of your (gross) income; you steward the ninety percent (90%). Although it all belongs to God, He entrusts you to be a good steward (business manager) over the ninety percent. It is a commandment (an instruction and the will of God) that we fulfill this obligation and plant it in the Kingdom of God. It is an act of obedience and obedience shows honor to God. The tithe is not a firstfruits offering. But it will usher in "The Blessing" which rightfully belongs to the tither. (See *Appendix E* for a Tithe and Offering Prayer.)

- **The principle of giving to God did not begin in the Old Testament** (Old Covenant/The Tanakh in Hebrew) but from the beginning of creation when the sons of the first family, Cain and Abel, brought offerings to God Genesis 4:3-7; Heb. 11:4. Some have restricted tithing to the Old Testament yet many things spoken in the Old Testament through God's prophets are still occurring and coming to pass today. The Old Testament conceals what is revealed in the New Testament. Without the Old Testament how will you know what God said has come to pass? Jesus Who brought the New Covenant said this, "Do not think that I have come to do away with *or* undo the Law or the Prophets; I have come not to do away with *or* undo but to complete *and* fulfill them," Matthew 5:17.

- **The tithe was given in the Old Testament and to date that has not changed.** He has never changed from receiving from His people, Mal. 3:10; Hebrews 13:8. There are other scriptures that support giving into God's house in the New Testament specifically to take care of God's people who work directly for Him so they may be freed up for prayer, study and services. In the book of I Cor. 9:13-14 it says, "Do you not know that those men who are employed in the services of the temple get their food from the temple?" 2 Cor. 9:6-11 shows how your seed will be multiplied back to you. I Cor. 9:18 talks about the preacher not taking advantage of *his rights and privileges* as a preacher of the Gospel. Also see Acts 6:2-4; I Thess. 2:9 it demonstrates that men of God who choose to work and preach so as to not burden the people, yet the people were not able to get the full impartation of the gifts from the men of God. They who worked did not have time to spend with God to receive what was fully needed for the people. In 2 Cor. 9:10 seed is provided to the sower. Also see Ezra 7:23-24; Numbers 18:21, 23 and Luke 6:27-38 which clearly states if you give it will be given back to you.

- **It is also best to tithe on the gross** (the amount of your income before deductions). This will include monies taken out by the government, the state and other taxes because taxes are obligations to delegated authorities in the earth for our well-being when the funds are handled correctly by the agencies our taxes are paid to. This protects our finances and closes doors to the adversary from robbing us in this area. One of those areas is owing the government money and having to deal with the Internal Revenue Service. In the book of Romans 13:7 it speaks about paying our taxes. But some governments take advantage of their citizens with usury and is addressed in the book of Nehemiah 5:1-13 NKJV. We can pray effective prayers regarding over taxation. (See *Appendix F* for a prayer regarding excessive taxes.)

- **Ninety percent of our income is entrusted to us for stewardship.** A part of it should be used for giving offerings, for savings accounts, paying taxes, investments for your future, living expenses, monthly obligations, grooming, reserve (for recreation, vacations, other) and helping others. Know because we tithe the Lord will cause the ninety percent to go even farther. One way He blesses the ninety percent is to supernaturally stretch or increase it in many ways such as to give you great discounts, connections, favor and miracles.

- **When we give the tithe and not Rob or Defraud God, He promises to Rebuke the devourer** for our sakes and not allow him to destroy the fruits of our labor, Malachi 3:8, 11. People are directed by God to give into to the House of God so there will be food/provision (spiritual and natural) in God's house. But keep in mind, because of our obedience to follow His instructions, the tithe protects our finances from spiritual attacks that manifest in the natural in the forms of poverty, lack, lost opportunities, debt and the like. The attacks on the Believer's finances by the enemy is to dethrone God's people from a position of dominion and influence in the earth. It is always wise to follow the instructions found in the Word that will protect what God is giving and imparting to you. (See *Chapter 4* under "Church, Ministry Leaders and Staff..." regarding His servants of God being compensated for their work and the tricks and lies the enemy uses to prevent them from receiving and others being blessed for giving).

- **Thanksgiving Offerings and Alms Giving also have blessings attached to them.** We do not give just to receive. We give because we have a heart's desire to share with others and do our part in advancing the Kingdom of God. We are to give to the poor and to those with an immediate need as a result of circumstances that have occurred in their lives. We should have a love for others and want to help if we are able to do so. We can also give to ministries God directs us to, so that ministry will be equipped and able to function and do for the people what God has commissioned. As we plant we share in the reward of their service in helping others. God says when we show love as He has commanded (instructed) in His Word He will repay us by blessing us because He desires to do so. He chooses to bless because we have honored Him in our reaching out to people He loves without being judgmental and having a prideful bad attitude. The offering causes increase in our lives. He uses our hands to bless others as He has others bless us. Matt. 22:37; Prov. 19:17; James 1:27, Exo. 22:22-23; 25.

- **Reasons why some do not give tithes and offerings.** Some feel they cannot afford it and this happens because of a lack of understanding of His ways and who He is. They do not trust Him to give it back multiplied or in any other form such as protection, healing, or answers to other prayers. They also do not realize they have an enemy the devourer (Satan) who steals, kills and destroys every chance he gets, John 10:10. The enemy will also try to convince you there is a right time to give. If you look at your circumstances and wait for the right time you will not sow and you run the risk of missing your window of opportunity, Ecclesiastes 11:4. When we are out of order, out of the will of God that opens the door for the adversary. Also, some argue it is Old Testament Law and they do not have to tithe because they live under grace with the New Testament. It is all a matter of how much you are able to trust God to come through for you. He said when you give the tenth it is holy, and it belongs to *His house*. Now, as you strive to take care of His house He will definitely take care of yours and in more ways than finances. In addition, when we give our tithe God blesses the remaining ninety percent because we honored the tenth as it is holy unto Him. Now we just only need to be a cheerful giver and exercise some faith.

- **The Lord gives us power to get wealth, it is a sign of His covenant with us,** Deut. 8:18. Whatever amount is entrusted to you, you have a responsibility to preserve it, grow it and extend the Kingdom of God. Realizing it is not only for you to be comfortable but for you to make a difference in other people's lives as you are led by the Holy Spirit. (See *Appendix G* to come into covenant with God, become a part of His family as well as position yourself to receive blessings as you give into His Kingdom.)

- **Praying in agreement is important,** especially when praying about finances. Finances involves an exchange to sell or buy which involves other people. Therefore, when operating in financial blessing and dominion a large part of God's Economic System is to come in agreement with someone else or with others corporately. When two or more agree, there He is in the midst, Matt. 18:19-20. All agreements should be based on the Word of God. True Biblical agreement is when all parties are standing on the Word of God and making it the center of the prayer.

- **Keep in mind to never make money a god. Anything that is exalted above God is idolatry.** If your money is positioned above God in a more important position it would be out of order and any time something is out of order doors are open for other problems to arise. *Remember money is only a tool and if we follow God's plan it will not control us but we will control it.* Then trust God to keep His Word and protect the rest that concerns our lives. Thank Him for giving us blessings, strategies, ideas and other streams of income as we increase His way. Maintaining money with the right perspective will keep balance and safety over our finances and in our lives.

- **People in the congregation have a kingly anointing**, to work and prosper. As they give into the ***priestly anointing*** on the man or woman of God they are freed up to pray, study, seek and receive fresh revelation from God to feed the people's "spirit man." In addition, as they go about doing good in the name of the Lord all those who are saved will remain in a place of strength, growth and prosperity. Also, *God has anointed many ministers of the Gospel in this hour to have both, a priestly and kingly anointing.* This is so they can manage and prosper in the blessings and businesses God is transferring to His Kingdom during these End-Times. God is prospering the people of God (not just the fivefold ministers) as He transfers wealth and creates opportunities and multiply streams of income. All He asks of us is to believe and keep Him first so He can continue in us. It is a known fact as you take care of God's house, He will take care of yours!

- **Repent for being in debt and receive God's forgiveness.** The Word of God says, "Keep out of debt *and* owe no man anything, except to love one another..." Romans 13:8. A "Biblical Financial Plan" (a godly financial plan/ budget/ instrument) would assist you with keeping your finances in God's order, with the wisdom of God to assist in managing your finances. In addition, it is important to maintain good records of your spending using registry books or sheets. Record all entries.

Have a good filing system for receipts, important documents such as statements, bank records, policies, deeds and so forth. (As stated above see *Appendix A* – the Biblical Financial Plan.)

- **Savings is a major part of God's spending plan.** It is used to set aside money for various reasons including paying or giving to yourself and some for your household. It is extremely important to set up savings accounts and designate them for short or long-term goals as well as being specific to name what the savings account is for.

- **Commit to something you can save consistently**. It is better to save less consistently than to save more inconsistently. *Always place saving at the top of your biblical financial plan or you may never save.* Spending habits change for people during the holidays, and summer months, therefore, if you have a business, plan ahead for those months. A biblical example would be the ant who gathers in the summer to make provision for the winter, Prov. 6:6-8.

- **It is a godly principle to take savings and pay off old debts.** You should not save money for yourself while you still owe money to others. One exception would be for emergencies. Save for the purpose of paying off your old debts first then whatever your specific goals are you can apply it afterwards.

- **Do not touch savings designated for long term goals** such as taxes, investments, large purchases unless it is a real emergency. This will safeguard the money so it can be used for what it was designated for. This is using wisdom.

- **Use accounts that do not have an ATM attachment** or some other method for making a quick withdrawal. *Make sure you designate your accounts for different purposes and exercise discipline to use it for the designated reason.* Again, if there is an emergency, that would be the only reason to disturb the account for anything other than its designated purpose.

- Money will decrease in value over a period of time. Therefore, it is wise to **transfer your money from cash to an asset that will increase in value** such as real property (home or commercial), stocks, bonds, mutual funds, gold, CD accounts, owning a business and other types of investments.

- **Our motive for giving and the measure by which we give play a key role in the**

rewards we receive. Luke 6:38 NIV says, "Give, and it will be given to you. A good measure, pressed down, shaken together and running over, will be poured into your lap. For with the measure you use, it will be measured to you." The Disciple's Study Bible says, "Our motives for giving usually determine the rewards we expect. Like a generous merchant who dispenses a heaping measure of grain, God pours out love and blessings to those who exhibit love for others by gracious giving. The greatest reward to a faithful giver is the joy of participating in Christ's ministry and seeing the results. Christ taught that rewards are gifts from God." [1]

- **No matter how much you save, unless you** *change your mentality about the amount you have saved it will never be enough.* Avoid thoughts and voices from others that say you do not have enough to save or to give. That is a trap from the pit to keep you in a poverty mindset and in bondage. If God made the provision then you have something to give and save. As you step out of the box and take control without fear but by exercising faith, you will give and begin to break the hold and mindset you are in and begin to prosper. Keep in mind you may have refrained giving for years out of fear so don't give up as you transition into doing things God's way. At the appointed time when the curses drop off and all God is aligning to bless you with are in place and in order, you will see the manifestation of His Word if you do not give up on your way to the promise.

• **When your income is lined up with godly principles, wisdom will follow.** As you continue with the Biblical Financial Plan your savings will become greater and your assets will increase and/or your liabilities will decrease.

Chapter 7

The Worldly Perception of Money vs. The Anointing of Multiplication

An unsaved or any saved person for that matter that embraces the world's economy leaves God out of the picture. Either they do not believe He exists or they do not believe including Him in their finances is necessary. They do not believe He could possibly contribute anything substantial to money matters or issues.

What the Bible says about Those Who are a Friend with the World, James 4:4

> You [are like] unfaithful wives [having illicit love affairs with the world and breaking your marriage vow to God]! Do you not know that being the world's friend is being God's enemy? *So whoever chooses to be a friend of the world takes his stand as an enemy of God.* (Emphasis added.)

Worldly people tend to trust in their own intellect for strategies, schemes, plots and management of money and business. How foolish it is to trust only in the knowledge of men when God has created the very tree from which man makes the paper that makes his money.

Many are unaware in the Bible God discusses money more than any other topic because He knew it would be a major issue for people since it is the primary way to exchange goods and services. He also knew many would try to steal and check others including the poor to acquire it.

God said, "He frustrates the devices of the crafty, so that their hands cannot perform their enterprise or anything of [lasting] worth. He catches the [so-called] wise in their own trickiness, and the counsel of the schemers is brought to a quick end" Job 5:12-13.

The world's system teaches people who belong to the Kingdom of God are not supposed to have wealth or even desire it because according to them money is evil. But in spite of them believing or telling others money is evil the ungodly uses plenty of it for all of their selfish gain, illicit sexual immoral businesses, films, and so forth.

Matthew 16:25-26 Speaks to Those who Try to Save Their Own Life of Comfort, at the Expense of Not Following the Righteous One,

> For whoever is bent on saving his [temporal] life [his comfort and security here] shall lose it [eternal life]; and whoever loses his life [his comfort and

security here] for My sake shall find it [life everlasting]. For what will it profit a man if he gains the whole world and forfeits his life [his blessed life in the kingdom of God]? Or what will a man give as an exchange for his [blessed] life [in the kingdom of God]?

The Lord is speaking in terms of choosing the higher life which is to live for Him and reap the benefits of being in the Kingdom of God as opposed to living the lower life, striving on your own, to gain on your own and missing the true riches of life.

The Bible does warn of the dangers of money being used for evil purposes. An area to guard your mind and heart from is the deceitfulness of riches. *People get caught up in the "perceived power" that comes with money.* Guard your heart by being selective of what you watch and listen to, including the world's media programs and news reports.

Also, guard your heart by being selective of who you fellowship with. Deceiving ideas can get into your heart through your eyes and ears and your heart can begin to change as you become more manipulative using impure motives to gain wealth. This leads to having sorrow that comes when one acquires wealth with means other than ordained by God.

The Bible says Judas, Lot, Achan and Ananias and Sapphira among others lied, stole, had a lustful eye for things and did whatever was necessary to acquire money and things. All of them had a miserable life and ending. They fell into the trap which changed their hearts and motives and they ended up with impure hearts which led to desires and ways that were not pure which opens doors for destruction.

When you wheel and deal with your plots and plans that are not godly but inspired by the adversary who influences you through your thoughts or through others, you are only allowing yourself to be deceived. Their worldly advice is designed to show you how to deceive others by using devices that are crafty and are full of tricks and schemes. So that "The rich rule over the poor, and the borrower is servant to the lender," Proverbs 22:7.

Now, because our Lord sees all, His Word tries the Word. To put it another way, no one really gets away with underhanded dealings, what you put out there, you will have to answer for. So, "Do not be deceived *and* deluded *and* misled; God will not allow Himself to be sneered at (scorned, disdained, or mocked by mere pretensions or professions, or by His precepts being set aside.) [He inevitably deludes himself who attempts to delude God.] For whatever a man sows, that *and* that only is what he will reap," Galatians 6:7.

Job 5:12-13 says,

> He frustrates the devices of the crafty, so
> that their hands cannot perform their
> enterprise *or* anything of [lasting] worth.
> He catches the [so-called] wise in their
> own trickiness, and the counsel of the
> schemers is brought to a quick end.

**John 12:47-48 explains, He does not Judge but
Saves, and His Word will Judge Wrongdoing,**

> If anyone hears My teachings and fails to
> observe them [does not keep them, but
> disregards them], it is not I who judges
> him. For I have not come to judge and to
> condemn and to pass sentence and to
> inflict penalty on the world, but to save
> the world. Anyone who rejects Me and
> persistently sets Me at naught, refusing to
> accept My teachings, has his judge
> [however]; **for the [very] message that I
> have spoken will itself judge and
> convict him at the last day.** (Emphasis
> added.)

The following passage demonstrates what
happens when you hear the Word of God but you do
not receive it into your heart where it becomes
rooted. *Because it is not rooted in your heart making*

a strong foundation to stand on, it in turn is stolen from you. This leads to compromising the Word and will of God, being unwilling or unable to stand for righteousness because you failed to guard your heart from outside voices and deceptive teachings and worldly influences.

The parable given in Mark 4:3-8 is regarding how we receive or don't receive God's written Word which is a seed when it is heard.

Mark 4:16-20 below is the Interpretation to Mark 4:3-8,

> And in the same way the ones sown upon stony ground are those who, when they hear the Word, at once receive *and* accept *and* welcome it with joy; And they have no real root in themselves, and so they endure for a little while; then when trouble or persecution arises on account of the Word, they immediately are offended (become displeased, indignant, resentful) *and* they stumble *and* fall away. And the ones sown among the thorns are others who hear the Word; Then the cares and anxieties of the world *and* distractions of the age, and the pleasure *and* delight *and* false glamour *and* deceitfulness of riches, and the craving *and* passionate desire for other

things creep in and choke *and* suffocate the Word, and it becomes fruitless. And those sown on the good (well-adapted) soil are the ones who hear the Word and receive *and* accept *and* welcome it and bear fruit -- some thirty times as much as was sown, some sixty times as much, and some [even] a hundred times as much.

When grounded in the Word you will be able to do things God's way. God's prosperity may come with persecution but not with sorrow, **"The blessing of the Lord –it makes [truly] rich, and He adds no sorrow with it [neither does toiling increase it],"** Prov. 10:22 and Isa. 53:4.

But when money comes without God and His ways a host of sorrows will accompany what you have because of how you obtained and made use of it. Therefore, without including God, yes you will acquire but it will bring bad success not good success at some point in your future.

When there is a lack of finances a worldly Greek mindset believes additional work will solve the problem because it will bring in additional income. This is logical and makes much sense to the natural mind. Though with it may come added stress, time away from your family, lack of proper rest, poor eating habits which will lead to poor health and a damaged social life or free time for yourself. All of these things will cause problems in other areas of your life. It is as if you solve one problem and add ten more. That is a part of the world's economic system to solving money problems.

Furthermore, please realize the problem is a spiritual one which is not commonly known or with knowledge of how to handle it. Since everything starts in the spiritual realm first, when things are out of order and out of balance in the natural, it is first affected in the spiritual realm then we see the results in the natural with our five senses. From there, we must choose to either change things by only using natural means, which rarely work, or by incorporating godly ways and means which will actually yield greater solutions.

When we choose God's ways and continue in Him He will turn the situation around. When we decide to stop exploiting others, using others for self-gain, stop taking each other for granted and so forth and make a sound decision to do things God's way this is what He says He will do:

Proverbs 22:22-23 NKJV says, "Do not rob the poor because he *is* poor, Nor oppress the afflicted at the gate; For the LORD will plead their cause, And plunder the soul of those who plunder them."

Ecclesiastes 2:26 NIV says, "To the person who pleases him, God gives wisdom, knowledge and happiness, but to the sinner he gives the task of gathering and storing up wealth to hand it over to the one who pleases God."

Proverbs 28:8-9 NIV **says,** "Whoever increases wealth by taking interest or profit from the poor amasses it for another, who will be kind to the poor. If anyone turns a deaf ear to my instruction, even their prayers are detestable."

Proverbs 13:22 says, "A good man leaves an inheritance [of moral stability and goodness] to his children's children, and the wealth of the sinner [finds its way eventually] into the hands of the righteous, for whom it was laid up."

The Anointing of Multiplication Makes the Difference in Our Finances

God said He will empower us to get wealth in Deuteronomy 8:18. He blesses us with all things and finances are a part of "all things." Jesus had the *anointing of multiplication* working in His life. One example of this was when Jesus/Yeshua multiplied two fish and five loaves of bread and fed over five thousand men and on another occasion, He took seven loaves and a few fish and fed over four thousand men. These numbers exclude the women and children that were with them who were also fed, Matt. 14:17-21; Matt. 15:36-37.

We must understand when we are saved and a part of His family, we can operate with the same anointing (power of God) that is His. When He paid the price at the cross, He received all authority (all power of rule) in heaven and on earth. In turn, He gave us, *by use of His Name,* the same authority on the earth, Matthew 28:18. Jesus also sent Holy Spirit, the angelic and the spirit of wisdom so we could operate correctly with His power (authority), John 6:63; Proverbs 1-7.

Therefore, we have the ability by faith to operate in the anointing of multiplication for finances in any situation, meaning we can apply it in our home, work place, ministry, business or for projects. Even though the early church (Followers/Believers, a combination of Jews and Gentiles, Galatians 4:3; Eph. 2:14) witnessed the anointing of multiplication, Jesus said, we would do greater works than He did by the Spirit of God John 14:12-13. God is the same yesterday, today and forever, Heb.13:8. Therefore, by faith we have the ability to operate in this anointing today at a greater degree!

The following is another example of the *anointing of multiplication* at work. Peter preached about the outpouring of the Holy Spirit and 3,000 Jewish people received their salvation (were saved) that day, Acts 2:36, 41. A few days after that 5,000 people were saved. We must remember the same principle of operating by faith applies in every area.

By the way, a person receiving their salvation and a life being transformed is a greater miracle than producing finances. In the eyes of God one type of miracle is not more difficult than another. *The anointing is what makes the difference and that is activated by our faith and our faith is activated by our love.* What am I saying? It goes back to the basic principle when we put God first and decide to do things His way (seeking first the Kingdom of God, Matt. 6:33) we will have the results we are looking for. All types of miracles and good things will be received for as long as our motives for certain things are pure in heart.

In order for the anointing of multiplication to be applied to your life you must activate it with the giving of firstfruits, tithes and offerings. Placing your giving into Jesus' hands through His storehouse is the same principle as when they placed the two fish and five loaves in Jesus' hands so when He gave thanks to His Father the anointing of multiplication was released.

When we are thankful coupled with our obedience to give in faith, as we release what belongs to God (the tithe which is holy unto God and various offerings including the Firstfruits offering) at the appointed time it will produce a harvest and is multiplied back to us. In the meantime, because of the decision to conform with His teaching the hedge of protection is strong. Then we go through our daily lives and are protected and given favor and experience breakthroughs until the harvest is fully sent.

In the natural, the world's way is to speak what you see with your natural eyes, so if you see lack you speak lack and accept it. *In the Kingdom of God, you line your words up with the Word of God and speak God's words in spite of any negative thing you see with your physical eyes.* The world cannot believe until they see. In the Kingdom we can believe by faith before we see or receive.

Words are spirit and containers of power, so when you speak them you will have what you say. Romans 4:17 NKJV says, "...God, who gives life to the dead and calls those things which do not exist as though they did..." So, we being of Him and in His family can call those things that be not as though they were and speak them into existence as long as our words line up with His will. And His will is found in His Word (the Holy Bible).

So in lieu of the negative report from your mouth you can change it and use godly positive words. For example, instead of saying "I can't afford it" say "I do not have the funds set aside for that right now but I will later" or you could say, "my money is already allotted for something else at this time so I'll make a note and take care of this at another time."

You can even quote scripture coupled with your words, "Even though I do not have what I need at the moment, God will supply all of my needs according to His riches in glory, Philippians 4:19. Through patience and endurance, continuing and doing what is right God will help you to be content in whatever state you are in until the change manifests, Philippians 4:11-13.

You are not lying, you are still admitting you do not have the funds for something but at the same time *you are not confessing you do not have any money nor will you ever have any for what it is you want to do or want to have.* What you are saying is not working against you in the spiritual realm. By confessing you will do it later you can activate something in the spiritual realm that is now going to move on your behalf if you believed it when you said it, Mark 11:23-24.

If you really did believe then you activated your faith and now God will move and use angelic forces if necessary on your behalf at the appointed time that is best for you to receive your request. Changing your words is one way that will stop demonic forces from moving against your finances through doors you opened with your words and gave space to them to operate against you.

The Bible says "death and life are in the power of the tongue, and they who indulge in it shall eat the fruit of it," Prov. 18:21. Be mindful of the words you put into the spiritual realm (the atmosphere) because angels and demons are waiting for instructions to move on your words. The angelic pick your words up to bring the manifestation when your words come from the Word of God, Psalm 103:20; Isa. 55:11. Demons pick them up when they are negative words full of doubt, fear and unbelief and bring those words to pass.

The Lord says to receive from God. So, freely receive favor, blessings, spiritual and natural gifts and the fullness of His abundance, John 1:16; John 10:10. It becomes important to choose to learn how to freely receive all God is offering you. Not only will it bless your life, but it will glorify God because it shows His Goodness! In addition, it will place you in a position to be able to bless someone else.

A quick note about the word *"free."* The world uses the word free as a bait to bring in business. Most people are aware it will not really be *free* and may even be costlier when all is said and done. Therefore, when the Lord says come as you are, freely receive the promises I have for you, because of the negative connotations associated with the word "free" many people including some Christians believe there has to be more to it or some kind of a catch. They believe it will be same sort of a trap set for them and once the bait is taken of something that was said to be free they find out the hard way it really was not free at all. So, they don't really trust the word free really means free when it comes to the blessings and promises of God either.

But for those who spend time with God through fellowship and learning of His ways and character, they will find the Kingdom of grace and love which belongs to the Kingdom of God is not like the world. God's love is a gift He chose to freely give to us. Our part is to believe His Word, receive it into our hearts and to be thankful we have a relationship with a living, *loving and caring heavenly Father who desires to freely give to us and for us to freely receive.*

> **The reward of humility and the reverent and worshipful fear of the Lord is riches and honor and life. Proverbs 22:4.** *(Emphasis added.)*

Therefore, you choose the perception you will have about money. Will it be from the world's Greek perspective or from a godly Hebraic perspective. Once you choose be prepared to receive according to your faith and choice!

God's Kingdom Flows with Generosity, 2 Corinthians 9:6-9 NIV and 9:10-11 AMP,

> Remember this: Whoever sows sparingly will also reap sparingly, and whoever sows generously will also reap generously. Each of you should give what you have decided in your heart to give, not reluctantly or under compulsion, for God loves a cheerful giver. And God is able to bless you

abundantly, so that in all things at all times, having all that you need, you will abound in every good work. As it is written: "They have freely scattered their gifts to the poor; their righteousness endures forever."

And [God] Who provides seed for the sower and bread for eating will also provide and multiply your [resources for] sowing and increase the fruits of your righteousness [which manifests itself in active goodness, kindness, and charity]. Thus you will be enriched in all things *and* in every way, so that you can be generous, and [your generosity as it is] administered by us will bring forth thanksgiving to God.

APPENDIX A

Biblical Financial Plan Sample ©

and Office Supply List

2.5 percent	**Firstfruits Offering** (Given at Rosh Chodesh at the beginning of each biblical month)
10 percent	**Tithe** (To the ministry Holy Spirit directed you to for equipping through His Word and training with ministry gifts that you should edify the body of Christ in His Kingdom)
2.5 percent	**Thanksgiving and Partner Offerings** (To other Ministries, especially during God's Feasts times; **Alms Offerings and Deeds** given directly to the poor or needy including widows and orphans
8 percent	**Savings** (Short and long-term Savings Accounts)
77 percent	**Obligations** (Responsibilities and open accounts)
100 percent	**Total Net Income**

GENERAL NOTES:

The **Biblical Financial Plan** (BFP) consists of Giving to God; Giving to yourself; and Giving to others.

A BFP worksheet could be used to list the items you need to take care of during a certain period in a given month. In addition, add in any sudden things that need attention that were not on your main BFP (the standard one you form your worksheet from). This worksheet would include the above and whatever additional items are being considered for issuance. The worksheet can also be filed for later reference if needed.

The Tithe is holy, it means the tenth. Holy also means set apart and special for God's use. Furthermore, it is best to tithe on the gross amount of your income from each of your businesses or your employment income(s). Tithing adds protection to all of your income. Because you are a *tither expect divine wisdom and favor* to cause increase and multiplication in your finances.

Amounts for *Savings and Offerings* are based on the net income. You should be able to increase both as obligations decrease. Also develop a savings chart that fits your household. Plan amounts to save from personal accounts and from business accounts if you are a business owner. Set funds aside for a reserve, long term goals, short term goals, emergency funds, major holiday accounts or whatever is necessary for your household. *Being consistent is key.*

Giving (planting seed) is a biblical principle that honor's God. For example, you give ten percent (10%) into His Kingdom and you steward ninety percent (90%). The ninety percent would cover your firstfruits, thanksgiving and/or partner offerings, saving accounts, taxes, investments for your future, living expenses, monthly obligations/expenditures, grooming, recreation, a reserve for helping others, your vacations and so forth.

Having a good filing system will save you time. It will prevent frustration of searching, missing scheduled time frames, wasting precious time and clutter. *Organization is always key.* It is a sign of excellence, good habits, good business methods and it will cause others to feel more secure and have a comfort especially if they are doing business with you.

Personal and Business documents should be filed separately. You can use the same file cabinet but separate drawers. Keep a master list in the top drawer of items in each drawer for easy location of files. Maintain good file cabinets that come with a lock. Bold tabs or labels will help you locate items quickly. *Some of the documents you may want to file are:* Personal family records such as a marriage license, birth certificates, social security information and cards, banking records (registry books, blank checks, canceled checks, bank statements), deeds, investment information, employment records, deeds, educational records, health information, general family info such as reunions, birthday list, functions, etc., memberships, DMV information, travel files, legal matters and so forth.

Use a 3x5 ruled index card for recording daily agendas, appointments, calls to make and projects if you prefer something other than storing daily agendas or notes on your electronics. It can be carried in a pocket or purse and checked off and discarded daily. It works beautifully as a quick reminder especially with all the demands most face today.

A reminder list, a separate order list, a grocery list and other types of lists for future use can be in separate files, places, on an electronic or one master file for various list. Also, if you like *schedules* to help with stay focused use them primarily as a guideline and reminder with flexibility and not as a rigid legalistic tool. Schedules can be very helpful.

**Supplies and Tools for Efficiency and
Professional Look for a Home Office or Business**

Executive or a very good comfortable supportive chair, especially if working extended hours; floor mat;

Desk of your choice – enough space on the desk to keep files and tools organized without clutter;

Landline telephone for office use; message pad. Cell phones should not be used close to your head without a corded headset or use of the speaker phone; Office mug, water;

Monthly planner, weekly appointment book, desk calendar or organizer;

Cooperate seal; safe; safe deposit box (optional);

Business and personal banking accounts; investments;

Letterhead; envelopes; business cards and holder;

Desk lamp; name plate (optional); desk trays (in box, out box, filing, pending); books; journals; dictionary; record keeping logs; mileage record book; Thomas Guide; Zip Code book or use electronics;

Post-its; 8x11 line pads; 5x8 line pads or journal for notes;

Pens; pencils; erasers; markers; pencil holder;

Letter opener; pencil sharpener; tape and dispenser;

Stapler; giant stapler; staple remover; staples (standard & heavy duty);

Liquid paper; paper clips; ruler; scissors; rubber bands (thick/thin);

Single, two and three-hole punch; ink pad and stamps re name/company;

Computer; printer; computer paper; ink or toner; program; internet;

Calculator; fax; copier scanner;

File drawers; file cabinets; hangers for file folders if needed; tabs; labels for folders and mailing;

Postage meter; postal supplies; mailing system; bulk mail; express services;

Office keys; desk keys; restroom keys (if any); misc. keys;

Receipt book; forms; proposal folder; info regarding business; employee manual;

Wall frames for photos and/or hang art in nice frames.

APPENDIX B

Withdrawal from My Heavenly Account

I operate in the Anointing of Multiplication that empowers me to withdraw blessings from my heavenly storehouse as I am:

Willing to be obedient to the Word of God;
Being faithful to His Word;
Exercising holiness by striving to live a sanctified life;
Seeking first the Kingdom of God (His way of doing things);
Giving firstfruits, tithes and offerings; and
Keeping vows that I made to the Lord

The prosperity demonstration begins in my life NOW from this night forward I will only think prosperity (wholeness – nothing missing, nothing broken and prosperous in every area of my life).

The rich substance of the universe instantly responds to my prosperous thinking. I am now rich in mind and manifestation.

Matthew 6:19-21 says, "Do not gather *and* heap up *and* store up for yourselves treasures on earth, where moth and rust *and* worm consume *and* destroy, and where thieves break through and steal. But gather *and* heap up *and* store for yourselves treasures in heaven, where neither moth nor rust *nor* worm consume *and* destroy, and where thieves do not break through and steal. For where your treasure is, there will my heart be also." Philippians 4:17, "Not that I seek *or* am eager for [your] gift, but seek *and* am eager for the fruit which increases to your credit [the harvest of blessing that is accumulating to your account]." I am to store up in my heavenly account as well as my earthly accounts, Prov. 13:22; Prov. 6:6; Deut. 8:18.

I decree and declare that my God has brought me into my wealthy place. I declare wisdom is my counselor and the Holy Spirit is my consultant in the handling of the money God has granted to me. Therefore, whatsoever I ask the Father in the Name of Jesus He will do it for me, Ps. 66:12 and John 14:13.

1 I decree and declare: $_____immediately;
    $_____now. $_____ weekly and
    $_____and more monthly as we factor in the
    Anointing of God on the way to $_____.

2   I lay hold of it by faith (when I pray I believe I receive it -
        Mark 11:24).

3   I come in agreement with another believer; Mt. 18:19,
        "...that if two of you on earth agree (harmonize together...)
        about whatever [anything and everything] they may ask, it
        will come to pass *and* be done for them by My Father in
        heaven."

4   I bind the devil and his forces by standing on Mark 16:17
        ("...in My name they will drive out demons..." Don't come
        back in this area, Mark 9:25.

5   I continue to loose the forces of Heaven Mt 18:18
        "...whatever I forbid *and* declare to be improper and
        unlawful on earth must be what is already forbidden in
        heaven, and whatever you permit *and* declare proper and
        lawful on earth must be what is already permitted in
        heaven." Therefore, I say go, prosperity angels and help me
        prosper by causing the money claimed, to come to me now.
        I say "Let there be" hundreds of thousands to millions of
        dollars from my heavenly account to my earthly accounts
        for the Kingdom of God and for me now in Jesus' name. I
        declare the blood of Jesus covers all of my bank accounts,
        assets and investments.

6   I praise God for the answer and the manifestation of the
        promises filled.

7   I will keep my confession lined-up with the Word of God
        and pray in my supernatural prayer language (tongues) as I
        am led in the matter until it manifests. I have financial favor
        from God!

8   Now Father, you have given me a great work to accomplish.
        I war for the releasing of finances and all resources that
        belong to me. I shall not and will not be denied. I shall not
        and will not accept substitutes. I call in resources from the
        north, south, east and west. I decree and declare that every
        resource necessary to fulfill this claimed amount that has
        been decreed come to me without delay, now. I thank you
        Father God for angelic assistance in the gathering of what is
        being sent to me in this time of harvest. I decree that the
        wealth of the wicked is no longer laying up for me but has

been released and is received now into my hands. Holy Spirit I commend into your hands those who hold onto my wealth longer than they should until they release what rightfully belongs to me. I command satan to cough it up, spit it out, release it, and let it go; it has no choice but to come to me. I decree and declare that my God has brought me into my wealthy place, Deut. 8:18. I declare wisdom is my counselor and Holy Spirit is my consultant in the handling of the money God has granted into my care.

Call those things which be not as though they were, Romans 4:17. To call in Greek means to summons, command and demand! Summons your harvest to come to you!

Money come to me Now! Godly change come to me Now! Favor come to me Now! I have financial favor from God and man Today! Proverbs 3:4.

I speak millions and billions into my accounts for the Kingdom of God. I speak millions and billions into my accounts for myself. Angels you are dispatched to go forth and bring the money for the Kingdom and me in Jesus' name, Amen!

Good Stewardship

A good steward is someone who does with his or her money what the Lord has said to do with it. Is not someone who is afraid to spend money or someone who spends it however they please. God is your source and He provided the money for you. He gave you the strength and the grace to work, the ability, wisdom, gifts and talents necessary to succeed.

Firstfruits, Tithes and Offerings are God's way of increasing you. God's agenda, for the finances He has entrusted to you, comes first at all times if you want to see the multiple increase in your life that God has for you.

It doesn't matter what time frames are before you, what bills need to be paid or even about your personal agenda or desires. None of these things supersede the purpose, power or order of God.

When God's purpose is first in your life regardless of any outside pressures or strong desires, keeping Him first places the Heavenly Father in a position where He can take care of you and meet all of your needs. Because of your obedience He will remember the covenant that He has with you.

Therefore, because you received His Son as your Lord and Savior and because you have a relationship with Jesus, and you are striving to obey His Word, the Holy Spirit and the prosperity and other types of angels are now in a position to move on your behalf and deliver unto you all that is needed and promised by God at His appointed time.

The Lord gives you power to get wealth (Deut. 8:18), it is a sign of His covenant with you. Whatever amount is entrusted to you, you have a responsibility to preserve it and grow it and extend the Kingdom of God. Realizing it is not just for you to be comfortable but for you to make a difference in other people's lives as you are led by Holy Spirit.

APPENDIX C

Firstfruits and Rosh Chodesh,
Head of the Month! ©

Rosh Chodesh is acknowledged and celebrated at the beginning of each new month according to the Biblical calendar, the calendar that God set in place thousands of years ago. **The principle of firstfruits is throughout the Bible.** This is one major way of keeping God first in our lives. It challenges us with how we position our hearts to align with His which will have much to do with the way the Lord responds to us. Why? Because the way the Lord responds to us depends on how we respond to Him. He said, come near to Me and I will come near to you, James 4:8.

To comprehend the significance of firstfruits, we must understand in life, there's something very special about the first (our first child, the first dollar of our business, our first date, our first car and so on). Just as we usually remember events that have a first such as the first man on the moon, or the first airplane, giving the first expresses honor.

When we choose to keep God first not only does it honor and please Him but it breaks us into a cycle of blessings and out of a cycle of curses (decrease). Seeking Him first, His Kingdom and His Righteousness ensures everything else is added to you, Matthew 6:33.

Giving firstfruits offerings is only one way to participate in keeping Him first; a way He has placed on this earth as a permanent mandate for our good. When we seek God by acknowledging Him, it gets His attention plus it reminds us we need Him in our lives and we belong to a loving Savior and Lord.

As we daily seek Him first it sets the tone for our day. **As we seek Him first during appointed Feasts it releases blessings (increase) and favor** and other benefits that aid us in this life to fulfill our purpose and inherit our portions. During God's yearly cycle of feasts they are also designed to break off oppression from the adversary Satan and draw us into the presence of God to dwell in His glory. He has designated these to bless us and make us a blessing to others as we continue to move forward in Him.

Firstfruits is one of the things God has designed to remind us we are not alone but we are a part of His family because of the covenant He made with Abram whom he later renamed Abraham, Gen. 12:2-3 and Gen.15.

There are different ways we can honor Him with a firstfruits offering: Give Him our time first as He then sets our day and helps us; giving money from the first of our harvest; from our income; from a promotion increase; and so forth. How much do we give? A portion of all that is your first and best. It does not have to be a large amount it is the willingness and obedience of thanking Him and keeping Him first to honor Him and to see our increase.

It will set the pace for the rest of the month. It is to be given to the house of God you are directed to by Holy Spirit. (Follow the leading of Holy Spirit as to which ministry is in your heart, especially those with knowledge of firstfruits.)

Other examples of firstfruits giving with increase are: Abraham was willing to put Isaac on the altar and God blessed Him greatly; Hannah gave her first son Samuel and God gave her many sons; The firstfruits spoil of the City of Jericho once it was conquered going into the Promise Land were given to the Lord and He blessed them with many more cities.

Also, Deuteronomy 26 tells us that when Israel entered the Promise Land and received their first harvest in the land, they were to put the first portion of that harvest in a basket and take it to God's sanctuary. *There, they were to give the firstfruits of their harvest to the priest and publicly declare the goodness and faithfulness of God.*

Another great example is, Jesus died as the Passover Lamb to redeem us and was raised as Firstfruits of those who have been redeemed from death to life and have become a New Creation in Him, I Cor. 15:3-6; 20. Furthermore, when God gave His Firstborn Son, Jesus/Yeshua the Messiah, the result was "bringing many sons into Glory..." (Hebrews 2:10.)

The Firstfruits is special because it is consecrated and set apart and considered "holy" by God. As with the tithe which is also holy, we are not to use it for personal gain but give it to God's house.

The firstfruits is not a contribution, offering or alms neither is it the tithes. As we know, the tithe is a tenth (10%) of our income which is given in obedience and honor to God. He has claimed the tithe as His own, Malachi 3:8-10.

For an example, when Israel brought in the full harvest, one-tenth of the whole crop was to be given to God as a tithe. *The firstfruits' amount was much less than that,* often just one sheaf of wheat. *Yet, this smaller portion opened the door to a massive blessing.* Firstfruits is a smaller portion which is given from the first of your income which sanctified the rest.

In addition, **the Bible describes three categories of giving.** In the book of Nehemiah 12:44 it says, "...men were appointed over the chambers for the stores, the contributions, the firstfruits, and the tithes, to gather into them the portions required by law for the priests and the Levites according to the fields of the towns..." The contribution, or offering, is anything given as an expression of thanksgiving to God as an Act of worship, in acknowledgement of God's blessing.

Specific blessings are promised for all three kinds of giving, but the fullness of blessing is released when we worship Him with all three.

The Three Categories of Giving is Described in More Detail in Nehemiah 10:35-39,

1. Firstfruits Giving, Nehemiah 10:35-37,

> And [we obligate ourselves] to bring the firstfruits of our ground and the first of all the fruit of all trees year by year to the house of the Lord, as well as the firstborn our sons and of our cattle, as is written in the Law, and the firstlings of our herds and flocks, to bring to the house of our God, to the priests who minister in [His] house. And we shall bring the first *and* best of our coarse meal, our contributions, the fruit of all kinds of trees, of new wine, and of oil to the priests, to the chambers of the house of our God.

2. Tithes, Nehemiah 10:37-38,

> ...And we shall bring the tithes from our ground to the Levites, for they, the Levites, collect the tithes in all our rural towns. And the priest, the son of Aaron, shall be with the Levites when [they] receive tithes, and [they] shall

bring one-tenth of the tithes to the house of our God, to the chambers, into the storehouse.

3. Nehemiah 10:39 tells the People to also Bring Contributions (or Offerings),

"...bring the offering of grain, new wine, and oil to the chambers where the vessels of the sanctuary are, along with the priests who minister and the gatekeepers and singers. We will not forsake *or* neglect the house of our God.

Those that participate in Firstfruits set aside each month a portion from their income as it is received and then at the New Biblical Month give it to the house of God they have been directed to by the Holy Spirit. (See below for a list of the biblical months.)

Just as giving God the firstfruits of our money releases His blessing on our finances, so giving God the firstfruits of our time releases His blessing on our time. Yes, the firstfruits principle still applies today. So, as we honor God with the first of our time, all of our time is set apart and we are positioned to walk in blessings all month. In exchange for our willingness to comply and remember to keep Him first as our source, His Word declares we will be blessed.

The reality of the blessings released by firstfruits giving is a powerful example to young and old alike. When all generations experience what it is like to live in the continual release of blessing, God is seen as a Good Father who loves and blesses all of His children. He is no respecter of persons.

When We Celebrate Rosh Chodesh (the new month) We Receive the Blessings of Firstfruits

1. We show honor, praise and thanksgiving to God for what He has done for us in the previous month. **Firstfruits honors God as our source,** which is a declaration that God has blessed us. Proverbs 3:9-10 promises that if you "honor the Lord with your capital *and* sufficiency [from righteous labors] *and with the firstfruits* of all your income; So shall your storage places be filled with plenty, and your vats shall be overflowing with new wine."

2. It is a time to worship, to inquire about the month ahead and to celebrate with God. **Firstfruits sanctifies (makes holy) the rest** of your income. "If the firstfruits is holy, then the whole batch is holy" Romans 11:16.

3. When we give Him our first (time, money, resources) we sanctify our whole month; and we position ourselves to receive His blessings. **Firstfruits releases the fullness of God's blessing.** Giving the first and best portion to the Kingdom of God will cause a blessing to rest on your household,

Ezek. 44:30. If we give Him our best then we can believe Him to give His best!

4. We set ourselves in a cycle of blessings when we honor what God appoints and honors.
The weekly Sabbath can be on any day because those in Christ/Messiah can rest in Him at any given time, however, God made a covenant with day number seven (7); the monthly Firstfruits giving; and the yearly appointed Feasts. Each one is designed for specific blessings as we acknowledge our Lord and Savior first.

As we are willing to comply with the instructions, in other words work the plans released from heaven to earth, **the willingness and obedience will release favor in our lives.**

The Word of God declares that the righteous shall be surrounded with favor as a shield, Ps. 5:11-12. Therefore, unmerited favor surrounds us like a shield and produces supernatural increase, promotion, restoration, honor, increased assets, real estate, greater victories, recognition, prominence, preferential treatment, petitions granted, policies and rules changed, and battles won that I didn't fight. *Favor is a direct result of "the blessing" that flows from obedience to Christ.*

According to Apostle Teacher Robert Heidler of Glory of Zion International Ministries in the book *A Time to Advance* written by Apostle Chuck D. Pierce along with Robert and Linda Heidler, he explains that "Rosh Chodesh" is an expression of the firstfruits principle. In order to live in the blessings of Rosh Chodesh, we must understand the concept of the firstfruits principle.

As we honor God by giving the first of the harvest we will recognize that *Firstfruits* truly is a major key to living in the favor and prosperity of God.

Biblical Months:

Month of Nissan-Abib	Mar/Apr
Month of Iyar	Apr/May
Month of Sivan	May/June
Month of Tammuz	June/Jul
Month of Av	July/Aug
Month of Elul	Aug/Sept
Month of Tishrei	Sept/Oct
Month of Cheshvan	Oct/Nov
Month of Kislev	Nov/Dec
Month of Tevet	Dec/Jan
Month of Shevat	Jan/Feb
Month of Adar	Feb/Mar

To obtain a Biblical Hebraic calendar visit:
www.elijahshopper.com

APPENDIX D

Why Should Christians Celebrate God's Feasts? ©

God is restoring to His Church the things that have been lost or stolen. He is bringing us into the fullness of the experience He originally designed for us to have so we could walk with Him. Experience His blessings and move forward into your destiny on His timetable.

The New Covenant (New Testament) reveals what was concealed in the Old Covenant (Old Testament). In the book of Jeremiah 31:33 and in Hebrews 8:10, 12 it is written God would make a *New Covenant with the house of Israel.* This was fulfilled in the New Covenant by Yeshua HaMashiach (Hebrew) for Jesus the Messiah (The Anointed One). Christians are adopted into this family when they receive the Messiah as their Lord and Savior.

In Matthew 26:26-28 during the Passover Seder or better known to Christians as the "Last Supper" Jesus/Yeshua had communion with His disciples. During that meal once Jesus had given thanks, blessed and broken the bread He told them to "take, eat; this is My body." The bread represented His body, then "He took a cup, and when He had given thanks, He gave it to them, saying, Drink of it, all of you; *For this is My blood of the new covenant, which [ratifies the agreement and] is being poured out for many for the forgiveness of sins."*

Furthermore, the Word/Bible quotes Jesus as saying, "Do not think that I have come to do away with *or* undo the Law or the Prophets; I have come not to do away with *or* undo but to complete *and* fulfill them…Whoever then breaks *or* does away with *or* relaxes one of the least [important] of these commandments and teaches men so shall be called least [important] in the kingdom of heaven, but he who practices them and teaches others to do so shall be called great in the kingdom of heaven," Matthew 5:17-19.

The Law, which are instructions, were fulfilled in the New Covenant. In doing so, the sacrificial killing of animals, the moral and ceremonial laws were all fulfilled. However, the sacrificial killing of animals is not practiced by those who know and understand it is no longer required since the final Sacrifice was received by Father God.

The Lord fulfilled the **Sacrificial Law** when He Himself went to the cross as the Passover Lamb of God. The Word of God says, "Therefore, purge out the old leaven, that you may be a new lump, since you truly are unleavened. For indeed Christ, our Passover, was sacrificed for us," I Cor. 5:7 NKJV.

The **Moral Law** expressed in the commandments were fulfilled with the Greatest Commandment. Where Jesus said, "You shall love the LORD your God with all your heart, with all your soul, and with all your mind." This is *the* first and great commandment. And the second *is* like it: *"You shall love your neighbor as yourself."* On these two commandments hang all the Law and the Prophets," Matthew 22:37-40 NKJV. You can also see John 13:34-35.

As a result, if we follow the instructions in the Greatest Commandment and practice it, we will have fulfilled all of the commandments throughout the Word including those in the book of Exodus chapter twenty. In practicing it, it is the same as walking in the fullness of what Jesus said. Furthermore, it means the Moral Law is for today.

The *Ceremonial Law* encompasses God's Feasts. Feasts are appointed times, days to meet with our heavenly Father allowing Him access which draws us closer to Him and thereby enabling us to accomplish specific things in our lives! These feasts occur at appointed times and seasons, a series of repeated cycles God put in the earth for mankind which were designed to align our lives with God's timing. When we honor God by meeting with Him the strategies of the enemy are broken. And in doing so this is one way we are equipped to move forward into our destiny. God put appointed times and seasons in the earth and no one has the authority to change them, Dan. 2:21; Acts 1:7; 2 Tim. 4:2-4.

Seven Feasts were given by the Lord have been recognized and observed by millions of Jewish people for centuries. Other feasts have been added by tradition or leadership. Because of the established covenant the feasts set in place by God have an open window for benefits when they are observed. In addition, according to God's Word on God's Biblical Hebraic calendar there are three feasts which must be observed by all whether they are of Jewish descent or a non-Jewish person that is a Believer/Christian.

The three main Feasts are: (1) Passover, in Hebrew Pesach; **(2) Pentecost**, in Hebrew Shavuot; and the **(3) Feast of Tabernacles**, in Hebrew Sukkot. These feasts have been set apart and are holy and they are to be observed every year by those who claim the God of Abraham, Isaac and Jacob as their God. His name YHVH, is the English rendering of the Tetragrammaton which is Yahweh or Jehovah. (See *God's Way and Knowing the King of kings* for additional information regarding the Lord.)

Why is it important for "true" Christians to observe the three main feasts? I say true Christians because many "religious" people call themselves Christians who have not received Jesus/Yeshua as their Lord and Savior and they are really not followers of His ways, teachings or instructions. Christianity is about having a Relationship with God Almighty not about religion.

One important reason Christians should celebrate the Feasts of God is that they are His. They are Biblical Feasts for those who receive His Word and desire to meet with Him on His appointed days. The whole cycle of feasts is designed to bring you into a fresh experience of God's Glory every year. The feasts did not begin under the Law because God established a detailed weekly cycle called Sabbath on His calendar at the foundation of creation in Genesis one when He said take a day to rest from your weekly labors and enjoy His blessings. Why is that and the other appointed feasts important - because they draw you closer to God. They are NOT legalistic rituals and a person will not go into outer darkness for not observing an appointed time. *The Feasts of God are designed to meet with Him, to keep you in His timing and to bring blessings into one's life.*

Gentiles who will observe God's feasts were also blessed. Jesus and the apostles all celebrated God's feasts. All those who learn to flow in God's yearly cycle will begin to gain a whole new sensitivity to the timing of Holy Spirit. This will cause you to begin to experience a new level of God's blessings. The early church celebrated the feasts for over three hundred (300) years before the Dark Ages and *for the last twenty years or so God has been restoring them back to His church.* Therefore, as Christian Believers "His Church" we were grafted into His family (Eph.1:5 and 2:11-13; 2 Cor. 5:17; and Gal. 3:24-25) and have inherited the Abrahamic Covenant (the blessings of Abraham). From the foundation this was part of God's plan, in Genesis 22:17-18 the Amplified Bible says, "In blessing I will bless you and in multiplying I will multiply your descendants like stars of the heavens and like the sand on the seashore. And your Seed (Heir) will possess the gate of His enemies. *And in your Seed [Christ] shall all the nations of the earth be blessed and [by Him] bless themselves,* because you have heard and obeyed My voice." Because of this we are enjoying the restoration of a valuable inheritance that had been stolen from the church. (See an explanation below).

Even though Christianity was birthed out of Judaism which is a Jewish religion, once a Believer, it should be noted Christianity is not a "Religion" but a "Relationship" a choice an individual makes to receive a way of life that brings one into a relationship with God Almighty, the Messiah, The Anointed One. *Christianity crosses all denominational lines, race, creed, ethnic group, color, culture, status or former religion because a Christian has become a new creature in Christ/Messiah through Salvation.* We are not changed from our race or even culture because we embrace what God did in sending His Son. However, we are changed in that we received His love and sacrifice that fulfills us and most of all gives us eternal life. After receiving Jesus/Yeshua as Lord and Savior it is our desire to honor His instructions from His Word the Holy Bible also referred to as the Torah; Tanakh; Old Testament and New Testament.

The First Four of the Seven Feasts given by God have Literally been Fulfilled by Jesus the Christ (Yeshua HaMashiach):

(1) *Passover* (aka Pesach in Hebrew; I Cor. 5:7; John 1:29; Lev. 23:5; Exo 23:14)

(2) *Unleavened Bread* (I Cor. 5:6-8; John 6:32-35; Lev. 23:6; Exo. 23:15)

(3) *Firstfruits* (I Cor. 15:12-20; Lev. 23:10; Exo. 23:16)

(4) *Pentecost* (aka Shavuot; Harvest or Weeks; Acts 1:8-9; Lev. 23:16; Exo. 23:16)

(5) *Trumpets* (aka Rosh Hashanah; Yom Trooah; Lev. 23:24-25)

(6) *Day of Atonement* (aka Yom Kippur; Lev. 23:27-28; Lev. 16 & 17)

(7) *Tabernacles* (aka Sukkot or Feast of Ingathering [Booths]; Lev. 23:34-42; Exo. 23:16)

The Five Tabernacles of God are as follows:

1. The Tabernacle of Moses, Exodus 40:33-35.
2. The Tabernacle of David, Psalm 63:2
3. The Tabernacle of Jesus, John 1:14
4. The Eternal Tabernacle, Rev. 21:3-4; Isaiah 4:5
5. The Church is God's Tabernacle, Acts 15:16-17

An Explanation of Why God's Feasts Have Not Been Celebrated by Most Christians Until Now:

During the season of *the early church which consisted of 90 to 100% of Jewish Believers who were followers of The Messiah experienced great power* with demonstrations of miracles through signs and wonders. The early church which met in houses were spreading rapidly, well into thousands of people attending them and honoring God's feasts, praying, giving, fellowshipping, teaching, ministering to one another and seeing signs and wonders because the presence of God was with them.

Then around 325 A.D. the Emperor Constantine of the Imperial Roman Empire or government decided after having a vision he thought was from God, even though he himself was a pagan and worshipped false gods, decided to make it a law everyone would become a Christian. He put this into law and if anyone opposed it they were to be killed. He proceeded to stop all of the house church meetings and bring everyone into buildings. He instructed the priests on what to tell the people. Tithing was forbidden, celebrating God's Feasts were removed, the presence of the Holy Spirit with the evidence of speaking in other tongues (I Cor. 14; Acts 2:4) was forbidden. Reading, teaching and ministering to one another was stopped. All instruction had to come from a few set-in leadership placed by Constantine.

Since the pagans became Christians against their will they refused to give up their worship to their idols so these false gods were incorporated into what we know today as the *Catholic Church* where the names of these idols were changed as they continued to worship their gods in the form of statues with names that began with the title of saint... He had the Roman priests teach God was done with the Jews and the Christians replaced them. Today this is referred to as "Replacement Theology" which is a lie that states the Biblical promises are no longer for the Jew but are given to the church. It is addressed in the book of Romans 11:11 NIV, "Did they stumble so as to fall beyond recovery? Not at all! Rather, because of their transgression, salvation has come to the Gentiles to make Israel envious. Furthermore, God has Promised Israel would return and it has (Ezek.11:14-20).

In this same chapter Apostle Paul addresses the Gentiles in case they decide to boast about having salvation given to them and try to replace the Jew. "Do not boast over the branches and pride yourself at their expense. *If you do boast and feel superior, remember it is not you that support the root, but the root [that supports] you.* You will say then, Branches were broken (pruned) off so that I might be grafted in! That is true. But they were broken (pruned) off because of their unbelief (their lack of real faith), and you are established through faith [because you do believe]. So do not become proud and conceited, but rather stand in awe and be reverently afraid. *For if God did not spare the natural branches [because of unbelief], neither will He spare you [if you are guilty of the same offense],"* Romans 11:18-21 Amplified Bible.

"And even those others [the fallen branches, Jews], if they do not persist in [clinging to] their unbelief, will be grafted in, for God has the power to graft them in again. For if you have been cut from what is by nature a wild olive tree, and against nature grafted into a cultivated olive tree, how much easier will it be to graft these natural [branches] back on [the original parent stock of] their own olive tree," (Romans 11:23-24 Amplified Bible).

"For He is [Himself] our peace (our bond of unity and harmony). He has made us both [Jew and Gentile] one [body], and has broken down (destroyed, abolished) the hostile dividing wall between us, by abolishing in His [own crucified] flesh the enmity [caused by] the law with its decrees and ordinances [which He annulled]; that He from the two might create in Him *one new man* [one new quality of humanity out of the two] so making peace. And [He designed] to reconcile to God both [Jew and Gentile, united] in a single body by means of His cross, thereby killing the mutual enmity and bringing the feud to an end," Ephesians 2:14-16 Amplified Bible.

Constantine also changed the Biblical calendar to the Gregorian calendar (January to December) which the Western cultures use to this day. Since God is the only One that can set the times and seasons God continued with the calendar He set in place. The Jewish people also continued with God's calendar and His Feasts. *They were chosen by God to be a holy nation of people – set apart and special.* They witness to the world there is a God in Heaven for the mere fact no empire, however great, has been able to completely destroy or annihilate them because of God's love and purpose for them. He has protected them and gives them great favor and divine wisdom to produce and achieve in all areas even though they are small in number. Because they are small in comparison to other larger nations they are considered a great nation because of what God has done for them as many of them have chosen to trust and honor Him and His Holy Scriptures.

The Lord still has a great plan for Israel and Jerusalem which belongs to them, Ezek. 11:14-20. Christians everywhere need to bless the children of Israel and pray for the peace of Jerusalem to honor God and what He has done for them and all those who receive Him, Psalm 122:6. *The Jew is responsible for giving us the Bible, many inventions, most of the electronics industry, the medical industry and even the military weapons that help this nation and the entire world. But most of all for giving us a Savior for our sakes, Who Himself came as a Jew, died (laid His life down), and in three days rose from the grave (through the power of Christ the Anointed One) as the Anointed King of the Jews, the Messiah. He will come again but this time as the Lion of the Tribe of Judah!*

So, the question still remains: "has God totally rejected and disowned His people? ***Of course not! ... No, God has not rejected and disowned His people*** [whose destiny] He had marked out and appointed and foreknown from the beginning..." Romans 11:1-2 Amplified Bible. "So too at the present time there is a remnant (a small believing minority), selected (chosen) by grace (by God's unmerited favor and graciousness)," Romans 11:5.

So, what is to become of the majority that has not received Christ? "So I ask, Have they stumbled so as to fall [to their utter spiritual ruin, irretrievably]? *By no means! ...*" (Romans 11:11). For it is written in Romans 11:25-28 Amplified Bible, "Lest you be self-opinionated (wise in your own conceits), **I do not want you to miss this hidden truth and mystery,** brethren: a hardening (insensibility) has (temporarily befallen a part of Israel [to last] until the full number of the ingathering of the Gentiles has come in, and so all Israel will be saved. As it is written, The Deliverer will come from Zion... they are still the beloved (dear to Him) for the sake of their forefathers."

APPENDIX E

Tithe and Offering Prayer ©

Father God in the name of Jesus and in the power of Your Holy Spirit, I welcome You this day. I stand in agreement with You, Your Word and those with me, Mt. 18:19.

Lord I honor You today with my firstfruits and/or my tithes and offerings and declare Your Goodness and Faithfulness, Proverbs 3:9, Deut. 8:18, 2 Cor. 9:8-11, Deut. 28:1-14.

I thank You Lord that You are forever mindful of Your Covenant with me, Gen. 12:3; Heb. 8:10,12. I thank You that You have chosen to bless me with spiritual and material blessings and an abundant life with my hearts desires, John 10:10 and Ps. 37:4. Blessings include wisdom, favor, grace, discernment, gifts of the spirit, divine connections, health, wealth, land and total restoration as You supply all of my needs according to Your riches in glory by Christ Jesus, Phil. 4:18.

Lord You gave me all authority over the adversary, Luke 10:19, therefore, I decree, declare and bind all of the enemy's evil assignments and plots sent to work against my finances. I am a tither and have tither's rights. So, I plead the blood of Your Son Jesus and draw a bloodline around my finances. Thank you that the angels have been commissioned to go forth and bring my finances to me.

You said in Mal. 3:11 You will rebuke the devourer for my sake and he shall not destroy my land. I receive Your blessings and increase as You enlarge my border and thank You that Your hand is with me to keep me from evil so it will not hurt me, I Chron. 4:10. I also repent if I have done anything to grieve Your Spirit and ask for forgiveness in Jesus' name.

You said if the thief is found out, he must restore seven times what he stole, so satan cough it up, release it and let it go now, Prov. 6:31. Lord as I pray You will hear me, as I pay my vows and decree a thing, it will be established for me and the light of Your favor shall shine upon my ways, Job 22:27-28. And I shall possess double and everlasting joy shall be mine, Isaiah 61:7. In Jesus' name, Amen.

APPENDIX F

Tax Prayer ©

Thank You Lord that my former Federal and State personal and business **taxes are forgiven and canceled** according to Luke 19:7-8 and Nehemiah 5:1-12 where *I have been cheated by usury* with interest and penalties by the tax collector, Luke 5:30-3; Ex. 22:25. Ps 15:5 says, do not put out your money to usury (taking advantage of a brother's distress to lend at interest ruinous to him) but rather give moderate interest as people deposit and use the services of a bank, Matt. 25:27 and Luke 19:23. Therefore, **I decree and declare this former debt is canceled in full** and I have a new and fresh start to bring all taxes current. *I thank you that the entire tax system changes for the people's good*, Mt. 17:25-26. **I bind the spirit of Eglon** that was used to tax and oppress me and I continue to **release the spirit of Ehud** which was sent to deliver me from excessive tax and oppression, Mt. 17:24-27. Where I was robbed all is restored one hundredfold to me. Angels go and do your part in closing out these cases. **I decree and declare any former cases are closed, in the Mighty name of Jesus!**

I will continue to bind, resist as well as block all future assignments from master spirits that work with every head of the spirit of the hydra that would attempt to use the IRS and the State Tax Board to bring recurring curses in this area of my life and ministry. Evil will not be able to come back into my life or the lives of my love ones in this area again (Mark 9:25) for Holy Spirit has released complete deliverance in this situation. **For it is written, who the Son has set free is free indeed,** John 8:36! In Jesus name, Amen.

> **You said, whatever I ask the Father in Your name you will do it,** John 14:13. Thank You Lord for listening and heeding me when I call to You; for hearing my supplication and receiving my prayer, Psalm 4:3; Psalm 6:9, I John 5:14. Thank You Heavenly Father that I can take refuge in You and that I can trust You to be a covering over me and for defending me, Psalm 5:11; Psalm 91. I went through fire and water, but You brought me to a place of abundance, a wealthy place, Ps. 66:12. According to Your Word I am to "keep out of debt *and* owe no one anything except to love one another" Romans 13:8.
>
> **No toil in paying taxes, Matthew 17:24-27 NIV; NLT:**
> Jesus spoke ... "What do you think, Simon?" he asked. "From whom do the kings of the earth collect duty and taxes – from their own children or from others?" "From others," Peter answered. "Then

the children are exempt," **("the citizens are free!")** "But so that we may not cause offense, go to the lake and throw out your line. Take the first fish you catch; open its mouth and you will find a large silver coin, take that and give it to them for Me and you."

Biblically **Tax Collectors** are seen as sinners, unrighteous, wicked, corrupt and sick people. Jesus said He did not come to call the righteous but sinners to repentance, Luke 5:30-32, Mark 2:14-17 and Matthew 5:46 NLT.

A P P E N D I X   G

A Prayer for Salvation and the Infilling of the Holy Spirit

If you are not a Born-again Christian with the Infilling (Baptism) of the Holy Spirit, or you are a Christian Believer and would like to rededicate your life to Jesus, say the following prayer. Afterwards, tell someone of the decision you have made regarding the Good News!

Dear Heavenly Father,

I come to You now, just as I am in the name of Jesus. Your Word says, "...Whosoever shall call on the name of the Lord shall be saved," Acts 2:21. And it says, "that if you confess with your mouth the Lord Jesus and believe in your heart that God raised Him from the dead, you will be saved" according to Romans 10:9.

I believe and confess now that Jesus (Yeshua) is the Son of God and He is alive today. I receive Him as my personal Lord and Savior. I ask for forgiveness and repent of my past sins and I choose to forgive others for their trespasses. Thank You Father God that Your Son has set me free from eternal darkness. I now declare that I am redeemed, I am healed, I am blessed, and I am whole. Therefore, I now have a renewed, abundant and confident life in Christ Jesus, the Messiah.

Father God, You said my Salvation would be the result of Your Holy Spirit giving me new birth by coming to live in me Romans 8:9, 11. So I ask You now for the Infilling of Your Holy Spirit as you have promised. Thank You for the gift to speak in other tongues, my spiritual prayer language that is unknown to man but known to God according to Acts 2:4 and I Corinthians 14:2. Now I bind the strong man that was sent to rob me and I plead the Blood of Jesus over my mind and mouth as I now release from my spirit my supernatural prayer language in Jesus' Mighty name. Amen! Give God Thanks!

The above Prayer is based on Romans 10:9-10 NKJV which says,

"That if you confess with your mouth the Lord Jesus and believe in your heart that God has raised Him from the dead, you will be saved. For with the heart one believes unto righteousness, and with the mouth confession is made unto salvation."

I John 2:2, 12 AMP says,

"And He [that same Jesus Himself] is the propitiation (the atoning sacrifice) for our sins, and not for ours alone but also for [the sins of] the whole world. ...*because for His name's sake your sins are forgiven [pardoned through His name and on account of confessing His name].*"

"Justified" – We are as if we never sinned! We are declared righteous, acceptable to God because of the Finished Work at the Cross where Jesus took our sins and gave us His Righteousness because in Him we have redemption through the blood! Hallelujah for a God Who Saves, Ephesians 1:7, Acts 4:12.

Salvation Scriptures:

Romans 10:9-10; John 3:14-17; John 5:24; Acts 2:21; John 10:9-18; John 6:44-51; Ps 51:5; Acts 4:12; Mt. 1:21; I Peter 1:23; Ro. 3:23; I John 1:9; Ro. 6:4; Acts 3:13-26; 2 Cor. 4:4; Eph. 2:8-10; Ro. 5:8; John 14:6; I John 4:9-10; John 3:3-6,15-16; Mt. 12:40; I Cor. 15:22; Acts 10: 40; Acts 16:31; Col. 2:6-7, Acts 15:11

Infilling of the Holy Spirit:

Acts 2:1-4; I Co. 2:4-5; Acts 10:44-48; Acts l: 5, 8; Acts 2: 39; Acts 11:16; John 4:23-24; Romans 8:6-17, 26-27; John 1:33; Eph. 6:18; Jude 1:20; I Cor. 2:14; I Cor. 6:19-20; I Cor. 14:2-15, 18; Luke 11:13; Ezekiel 11:19; I Cor. 12:7-11; Eph. 5:18; John 16:13; Gal. 5:22-23; Isaiah 11:2-3; Romans 6:1-11

NOTES

Chapter One:
Biblical Economics Assures Financial Progress and
Good Success

1. Joseph Prince, *Destined To Reign, Devotional.*
   Tulsa: Harrison House, 2008

2. Chuck D. Pierce, *A Time to Advance.* Denton:
   Glory of Zion International, Inc., 2011

Chapter Two:
Prosperity is a Part of God's Kingdom

1. Chuck D. Pierce, *A Time to Advance.* Denton:
   Glory of Zion International, Inc., 2011

2. ibid

3. Joseph Prince, *Destined To Reign, Devotional.*
   Tulsa: Harrison House, 2008

4. ibid

Chapter Three:
What the Bible Really Says About Money, the
Transfer of Wealth and More

1. Mark A. Beliles and Stephen K. McDowell,
   America's Providential History. Charlottesville:
   Providence Foundation, 1989, 1991

Chapter Five:
Recognizing and Overcoming a Poverty Spirit and
Mindset

1. Valerie K. Brown, *Miseducation of the Christian.*
   Lake Mary: Creation House, 2007
2. Disciple's Study Bible, NIV Footnote. Nashville:
   Holman Bible Publishers, 1988

Chapter Six:
Removing Debt God's Way Using Spiritual and
Natural Instruments

1. Disciple's Study Bible, NIV Footnote. Nashville:
   Holman Bible Publishers, 1988

About the Author

Audrey L. Dickey, D.Min., Ph.D. is an apostle, prophetic voice, author and conference speaker. She ministers the Word and counsels prophetically to advance the fivefold ministry in the Kingdom of God. Her books include spiritual warfare strategies and tools for marriages, families, finances, everyday life experiences and Kingdom business. Since her youth she has seen signs and wonders, healings and prophecies come to pass through the power of God. Dr. Audrey holds a Doctor of Philosophy in Religious Studies and a Doctor of Ministry with emphasis in Biblical Counseling from FICU in California. She is also a member of the American Association of Christian Counselors (AACC). She along with her husband, Robert L. Dickey, Ph.D. received a vision to establish an international apostolic, prophetic ministry. They are the founders and CEO's of Christian Love Glory International Center as well as the founders and apostles of Christian Love Fellowship Church, Inc. This Fivefold multi-cultural ministry includes covenant restoration of the One New Man and will oversee designated marketplace businesses. Drs. Robert and Audrey Dickey have five children and make their home in Los Angeles, California.

To Contact the Author:
Dr. Audrey L. Dickey
P. O. 48288
Los Angeles, CA 90048
www.robertandaudreydickeyministries.org